THE DUNDEE TEXTILES INDUSTRY
1960–1977

THE DUNDEE TEXTILES INDUSTRY 1960—1977

Decline and Diversification

W Stewart Howe

British Library Cataloguing in Publication Data
Howe, W. Stewart
The Dundee textiles industry, 1960 1977
1. Textile industry—Scotland—Dundee—History
I. Title
338.4'7... I. Howe...
ISBN 0 08 028454 X

ABERDEEN UNIVERSITY PRESS

First published 1982
Aberdeen University Press
A member of the Pergamon Group

© W Stewart Howe 1982

British Library Cataloguing in Publication Data
Howe, W. Stewart
The Dundee textiles industry, 1960–1977.
1. Jute industry—Scotland—Dundee—History
I. Title
338.4′767713   HD9156.J7
ISBN 0 08 028454 X

PRINTED IN GREAT BRITAIN
THE UNIVERSITY PRESS
ABERDEEN

CONTENTS

for Andrew and Alison
despite whom this work was completed

Acknowledgements

No work such as this could have been completed without the
help of numerous people, and I have been particularly fortunate in the co-operation which I have received from others
over the past five years.

In the first place the research project of which this book is
a result received financial assistance from two sources. The
Research Committee of Dundee College of Technology provided
financial assistance throughout the duration of the project
(1976-1981), and the Houblon-Norman Fund of the Bank of
England made an award in respect of the year 1976. The
research could not have been carried out without such assistance, for which I am most grateful.

As in the case of all academic writers, I owe an intellectual
debt to the many people with whom I have discussed my
research. Mr. Stuart McDowall, Senior Lecturer in Economics
at St. Andrews University, and Professor Douglas Garbutt,
Dean of the Faculty of Management and Social Studies at Dundee
College of Technology, were respectively my Director of
Studies and Second Supervisor in regard to the Ph.D. research
project on which this study is based. To each of them I
would express my sincere thanks both for their time taken in
discussing the material and in generally stimulating my
thoughts in this area. Professor D.P. O'Brien of Durham
University was also an invaluable source of constructive
criticism on the draft chapters of the work; and I must
additionally acknowledge the help of my former Departmental
colleague at Dundee College of Technology, Mr. J.D. Mushin,
in introducing me to the facilities available on the College's
computer.

A study such as this obviously relies heavily upon a considerable amount of new information. I am extremely grateful to
the staff of Dundee College of Technology library for their
help in obtaining a large number of national and international publications for me and also other sources of data on the
U.K. textile industries. I have also received considerable
help from the staff at the National Library of Scotland and
the Scottish Office, and from those at the Companies Regis-
tration Offices in London and Edinburgh. The data, particularly in Chapters 3 and 4 of the book, were processed on the
College's DECSYSTEM-20 computer, and the existence of this
facility and the help of the Computer Centre staff is grate-
fully acknowledged.

With regard to information on the jute and polypropylene
industries my sincere thanks are due to a large number of
senior businessmen in the firms in the industries who gave
generously of their time to help in my research. Their traditional wish is to remain individually anonymous, but the
following list of firms comprises those whose executives (on
occasion more than one within a single firm) helped in the
research. Individuals mentioned by name are those, normally
retired, who helped in their personal capacity.

Association of Jute Spinners and Manufacturers
Sir Herbert Bonar
Caird (Dundee) Ltd.
Co-operative Wholesale Society (Taybank Jute Works)
Don Brothers Buist Ltd.
Wm. Halley & Sons Ltd.
Hardie & Smith Ltd.
A. & S. Henry Ltd.
Low & Bonar Group Ltd.
Malcolm, Ogilvie & Co. Ltd.
Mr. Lewis Robertson
H. & A. Scott Ltd.
Scott & Fyfe Ltd.
Scott & Robertson Ltd.
The 'Shell' Transport and Trading Co. Ltd.
Sidlaw Industries Ltd.
Dr. H.P. Stout
Thomas Thomson Ltd.
Thomson, Shepherd & Co. Ltd.
Union of Jute, Flax and Kindred Textile Operatives
Victoria Spinning Co. Ltd.

A very special word of thanks must go to Mrs. P. Sawers who
cheerfully and efficiently undertook the onerous task of
preparing the typescript of the book in "camera-ready" form.
The final appearance of the text is very much due to her
skill and willingness to endure the many burdens of the
typist under these demanding conditions.

Finally, but by no means least of all, I would express my
sincere thanks to my wife Kerrie for her patience while this
study was being undertaken. My absences from the home not
only in body but even more frequently in mind have been nobly
borne - if only in the hope that this will be the last piece
of research to be conducted for some time. Such patience and
support is much appreciated.

INTRODUCTION

The aim of this text is to report on the conducting of an
economic organisation study of one particular economic
market - referred to broadly as the Dundee industrial textiles
industry. The study has therefore been carried out at the
partial microeconomic level, and has been conducted within
the framework referred to in industrial economics as
structure, conduct and performance analysis (Bain, 1967).
The analysis and conclusions in the study are based not only
upon the assembled data (some of them hitherto unpublished,
others being used in a novel manner) but also upon a large
number of interviews held with senior management in the
industry.

So far as the author is aware no other study of this aspect
of the Dundee industrial textiles industry has been carried
out. Earlier or contemporary work by Leveson (1973) and by
McDowall and Draper (1978) has either been concerned with
management aspects of the industry, or with using the jute
industry as an example of a separate individual economic
phenomenon.

The topic of this study is the Dundee industrial textiles
industry. The epithet Dundee serves to stress not only the
high degree of geographical concentration of the traditional
U.K. jute industry in that city (some 90% of spinning and
weaving of jute in the 1960's), but also the vital importance
of the jute industry to Dundee: it accounted directly for
some 50% of the city's employment within living memory
(Carstairs, 1968). Unlike many industry studies this is, at
least initially, one of decline rather than of expansion -
indeed of dramatic decline in the traditional work of jute
spinning and weaving. But it is also an account of survival,

in that it contains an analysis of the diversification of the
existing "jute" firms both into man-made fibres (predominantly
polypropylene) and into other market areas in some cases less
related to the original industry. References in the title and
elsewhere in the study to the Dundee industrial textiles
industry thus cover both the traditional market for jute and
the new industrial textiles etc.

The structure, conduct and performance approach accounts for
the framework of the study. Chapter 1 comprises a historical
introduction to the jute industry, and outlines the condition
of the market in 1945. Structure refers to the main environ-
mental features of an industry, and Chapter 2 contains an
analysis of the major changes in this market over the post-
1945 period, and in particular over the period from the mid
1960's to 1977. The aim of this material is to provide an
account and an analysis of the major structural changes in the
industry over these years with a view to arriving at conclusions both as to the forces which caused the changes and also
the impact which the changes had upon competition, efficiency
and resource allocation in this particular market.

Chapter 3, under the heading of Diversification, examines in
detail the conduct or behaviour of firms in the market: what
Bain (1967, p.9) identifies broadly as "patterns of behaviour
that enterprises follow in adapting or adjusting to the markets
in which they sell (or buy)". Since diversification undoubtedly embraces the major company strategy in this process of
adaptation or adjustment in this particular market, the major
emphasis in analysing market conduct is placed upon it, and
other features such as product improvement and technological
adjustment are subsumed within it.

Market performance is measured and analysed in Chapter 4 under
a number of headings, with reliance being placed very largely
upon a quantitative approach. The purpose of the analytical
section of the chapter is to offer an economic interpretation
of the purely statistical findings, and to compare these
results with the general body of similar empirical studies in
industrial economics.

The final chapter offers conclusions on efficiency and resource
allocation across the industry, drawing upon the preceding
three chapters in particular.

One of the major problems involved in carrying out empirical
research in industrial economics is the degree of economic,
or more particularly econometric, sophistication which is

held to be appropriate; and with this is inevitably linked
the issue of a case-study vis-à-vis large-scale statistical
approach to any issue. It is in some way a question of
balancing the quest for detail and generality - for "realism"
and the drawing of formal conclusions. This issue has been
responsible for a significant division of approaches to broadly
similar topics in industrial economics. On the one hand there
are those who favour a more detailed case-by-case approach to
arriving at conclusions on industry behaviour. On the other
hand there are those who would point out that the general
validity of conclusions must lie in the use of cross-sectional
and time-series analysis of large volumes of statistical data,
and that it is not necessary to have a detailed regard to the
highly specific "facts" of each individual case. The problem
of choosing between these two approaches was put clearly by
Alfred Marshall (1920).

> "If we include in our account merely all the
> conditions of real life, the problem is too
> heavy to be handled; if we select a few,
> then long-drawn-out and subtle reasonings
> with regard to them become scientific toys
> rather than engines for practical work."

The relative merit of the large-scale cross-section or time-
series study would appear to lie in the greater ability to draw
general conclusions based upon statistical analysis of a large
number of observations. Such conclusions may be of more value
simply because they derive from an overall analysis of an
economic issue, or because the large numbers involved allow
more "degrees of freedom" in statistical analysis. The value
of the case-by-case approach lies in a greater acquaintance
with the facts of a particular industry, a greater appreciation
of the quality (or otherwise) of the statistics, and a more
secure base upon which to arrive at meaningful economic conclusions - albeit about a smaller part of the economic world
involved.

One would like to think that time would eventually bring about
a union of the two approaches, or that each would be regarded
as being valid in its own right or for its own particular
purpose. This does not, however, appear to be the case at the
present time. One cannot, moreover, rule out the influence of
personal preference on the part of individual authors. Some
writers (Johnston, Buxton and Mair, 1971) simply prefer to work
at a level which incorporates a degree of institutional detail -
feeling that "statistical analysis does not always catch the
spirit and the bustle of industry when it is taking its pulse

and temperature". Others (Downie, 1958) appear to have reservations about the value of the individual-industry study
"whose mountain of descriptive material is far too intransi-
gent to be formed and informed by a theoretical framework".
Having had experience, as a co-author of published studies,
of two very different approaches to the analysis of the economic impact of U.K. competition-policy legislation, the author
has attempted in this study to combine the advantages of each
broad approach. The study is constructed at a point along the
spectrum of formal analysis and description which will accom-
modate a sound economic framework, statistical analysis and
some institutional detail. It is "historiate", to use the
term adopted by Phelps Brown (1972), but operates within the
structure, conduct and performance framework of analysis
accepted in industrial economics. This analysis is based upon
examining the principal elements of market structure (concentration etc.), market behaviour and economic performance, and
involves establishing relationships between these areas. Such
analysis enables one to emphasise the most appropriate historical details, to pay attention to the most relevant current
characteristics of a market, and to draw more general conclusions for further analysis than is often possible from a purely
historical account of an industry's development or decline.
At the same time such a mode of analysis allows one to
explore further than would be possible within the confines of
formal microeconomic analysis. It is within this industrial
economics framework that the following analysis has been
carried out, and on the basis of which the final conclusions
are offered.

Thus the purpose of this study is not simply to set out to
describe what happened to the firms which at one time constituted the Dundee jute industry over a particular period of
adjustment to new markets and technology. This in itself is
of course important; and much time has had to be spent
operating in what have been factually largely uncharted
waters. The study, however, sets out to do more than this.
It seeks in particular to do three things. First, to offer
an explanation for the events whose course is traced. Second,
to test the events of the industry's recent past against various hypotheses founded upon the theory of micro-economics or
industrial economics. Third, to assess the resource allocative
implications of the findings. Thus in respect of changes in
markets and industry structure, an explanation is sought for
the changes in the pattern of concentration in the industry,
the type of price leadership which at one stage emerged is
compared with that which an understanding of economic theory
would lead one to expect, and an assessment is made of the

impact of such changes and behaviour upon the efficiency of
the industry over the period. As regards diversification, an
explanation for the poor returns to this corporate strategy
is attempted, certain hypotheses regarding diversification,
profitability, size and growth are tested statistically, and
again some attempt is made to assess the impact of the strategy upon resource allocation in the industry. In particular
in Chapter 4, dealing with market performance across a number
of dimensions, a range of statistical tests is carried out on
variables such as profitability, growth, productivity, capital
investment, and research and development expenditure. The
purpose of this is not only to describe, but to compare the
behaviour of our group of firms with findings on these phenomena relating to manufacturing industry as a whole, and to
offer explanations for any observed differences. The hypothesis here is that our group of firms would be expected to
conform to behaviour observed in much larger samples in cross-
sectional and time-series analysis. The strands of thought
brought out in respect of individual aspects in Chapters 2, 3
and 4 are all gathered together in Chapter 5 in a final attempt
to explain the happenings in this industry over the period
studied, to compare the findings of our industry with those
relating to the U.K. manufacturing sector as a whole, and to
offer conclusions on the degree of economic efficiency within
the industry.

References

Bain, J.S. (1967). Industrial Organization, 2nd ed. Wiley,
New York.

Carstairs, A.M. (1968). The nature and diversification
of employment in Dundee in the twentieth century. In S.
Jones (Ed.), Dundee and District. British Association,
Dundee. p.320.

Downie, J. (1958). The Competitive Process. Duckworth,
London. p.20.

Johnston, T.L., N.K. Buxton and D. Mair (1971). Structure
and Growth of the Scottish Economy. Collins, Glasgow.
p.100.

Leveson, J.H. (1973). Industrial Organisation of the Jute
Industry. College of Technology, Dundee.

McDowall, S. and P. Draper (1978). Trade Adjustment and the
British Jute Industry. Fraser of Allander Institute,
Glasgow.

Marshall, A. (1920). Principles of Economics, 8th ed.
Macmillan, London. pp.460-1.

Phelps Brown, E.H. (1972). The underdevelopment of economics.
Econ. Jour., 82, 9.

CHAPTER 1

HISTORICAL BACKGROUND TO 1945

INTRODUCTION

The purpose of this chapter is twofold. First, to offer a
brief economic history of the U.K. jute industry from its
origins in the 1830's until 1945. Second, to emphasise some
of the most important economic characteristics of the industry
in the post World War II period so as to lay the foundation
for the analysis of changing markets and industry structure
over the period 1960-1977 in Chapter 2.

THE ORIGINS OF THE U.K. JUTE INDUSTRY

Some form of historical introduction would appear to be necessary to any economic analysis of the Dundee jute industry.
More than most industries it has been an economic prisoner of
historical developments largely beyond its control. Thus two
authors (Carstairs and Cole, 1960) more recently refer to its
development as "a catalogue of instability and frustration",
and highlight the rapid war-time expansions in the 19th
century, and long-term contraction punctuated by occasional
hectic prosperity within living memory. As a particular
example of this tendency one historian (Gauldie, 1969, p.xv),
writing of the conditions of the 1850's and 1860's, comments:

> "At the height of the boom any man who could
> buy or rent a tumbledown mill could make a
> fortune. After the boom, shrinking markets
> and wildly fluctuating costs produced a sit-
> uation in which entrepreneurial skills could
> have little effect on the downward trend of
> the industry".

To appreciate the early development of the jute industry it is
necessary to know something of the economic history of cotton
and linen or flax (Rimmer, 1960). Flax spinning and weaving
appears to have been in its beginning a peasant occupation.
But by the end of the seventeenth century it was both a rural
and urban trade; although at this stage the final product was
a rather rough and heavy cloth, and finer linens were imported
from the Continent. The growth of the linen industry on any
scale in the eighteenth century was dependent upon imports of
flax and yarn, and therefore tended to be concentrated in the
north of the country (including the Clyde valley in Scotland),
based upon Baltic imports. The histories of cotton and linen
were closely intertwined - literally so in the case of union
goods with a flax warp and cotton weft. As an example of this
interrelationship, the rise in the price of cotton in the mid
eighteenth century as demand went ahead of supplies gave linen
manufacturers an opportunity to expand into new markets; and by
the last quarter of the century the two industries appear to
have been of roughly equal size (Dean, 1965). However, in the
closing decades of the eighteenth century increased supplies of
raw cotton from the Southern States of America, and the earlier
technical innovations in the spinning and weaving of cotton,
gave the latter an advantage over linen in both home and export
markets. These changes resulted in cotton displacing linen
manufacturing on the west coasts; and Lancashire, North-east
Ireland and the Clyde valley declined as linen producing centres, tending to specialise in cotton. It was these same
changes which opened up opportunities in the linen trade for
centres such as Darlington, Leeds and Dundee.

Historically the jute industry grew out of the linen or flax
spinning and weaving trade. There was an established flax industry in Dundee in the late eighteenth century; and although,
as mentioned above, linen was superseded by cotton in some markets with a consequent downturn of the industry in parts of the
economy, the coarse linen trade of Fife, Angus (then Forfar-
shire) and Perthshire prospered. The markets catered for were
sail canvas, "soldiers' sarking" (i.e. coarse linen shirts for
the army) and the clothing for negro slaves in America. Dundee
appears to have been the focal point of this prosperity, and in
the late eighteenth century rapidly became the centre of what
had hitherto been a more dispersed domestic linen industry in
its hinterland. What it may have lacked in water power it made
up for as a thriving commercial centre. According to Peter
Carmichael's autobiography, between 1815 and the early 1830's a
sum of not less than £250,000 had been spent on the harbour; by
1833 the Earl Gray dock was under construction; there was a
ferry across the Tay, a paddle vessel running to Perth, and a

daily coach to Glasgow; and the Dundee to Newtyle railway
was the first to be opened in Scotland in 1851 (Gauldie,1969,
p.59). Dundee was well placed to receive Baltic flax; and
while in 1815 (the first year for which such figures are
available) Dundee imported 1,221 tons of flax (7% of the total
U.K. figure), by 1836 the figure had risen to 30,653 tons -
40% of U.K. imports. Between 1816 and 1833 the population of
Dundee expanded from 30,000 to 50,000; and over the period
1811-1835 30 flax spinning mills were opened. The period of
the early nineteenth century was thus one of general prosperity
for the traditional Dundee textile industry; and it was into
this environment that jute was introduced.

THE RISE OF THE JUTE TRADE

Warden (1867, pp.66-9), in his immensely detailed study of the
linen trade, tells of the tentative introduction of jute into
this country at the end of the eighteenth century and of its
use in the manufacture of door mats, ropes etc. The expansion
of this experience led to its use in a form of carpeting at
Abingdon in Oxfordshire; and in the early 1830's similar
experiments were carried out in Dundee. The substitution of
jute for flax and hemp was particularly a possibility in
Dundee, as compared with other linen centres such as Leeds,
because of Dundee's specialisation in the coarse end of the
trade. The introduction of jute spinning appears to have been
complicated at this time because only at this date was flax
spinning by power being introduced, and it was anticipated
that the jute fibre would present additional difficulties in
the application of power spinning. There was also the problem
of securing the acceptance by users of goods made partly or
wholly of the new, inferior jute yarn. The commencement of
jute yarn production is usually dated from 1833 at the Chapel-
shade works of Balfour & Meldrum - on the site now occupied
by Dundee College of Technology (Woodhouse and Brand, 1934);
and stimulated by the acceptance by the Dutch Government of
jute in the place of flax tow in a large coffee bagging contract in 1838 the jute industry began a period of considerable
expansion. Some indication of this can be gained from data
relating to Dundee jute imports.

TABLE 1.1   Jute Imports into Dundee (Tons)

1832	182	1843	4,858	1854	16,590
1833	300	1844	5,515	1855	25,894
1834	828	1845	8,313	1856	31,031
1835	1,222	1846	9,230	1857	24,342
1836	16	1847	6,966	1858	30,086
1837	171	1848	8,905	1859	38,405

TABLE 1.1 cont'd

1838	1,136	1849	12,142	1860	36,965
1839	2,411	1850	14,080	1861	35,716
1840	2,745	1851	16,928	1862	38,277
1841	2,661	1852	16,983	1863	46,983
1842	2,740	1853	15,400		

Source: Warden, A.J. (1867). The Linen Trade, Ancient and
         Modern, 2nd ed. Longmans Green, London. pp.76 and
         633.

The jute industry expanded in and contributed to the general
prosperity of a city which was becoming a major commercial
centre: a city where trade in 1851 exceeded that of any Scots
town except Glasgow according to a study of the period (Lenman,
Lythe and Gauldie, 1969, p.7).

By the late 1850's jute had begun to overtake flax in importance as measured by tonnage imports; and by 1863, when jute
was enjoying the full benefits of the American Civil War (1861-
65), the respective tonnages of flax and jute were 23,474 and
46,983 (Warden, 1867, p.633). This was also a period of considerable mechanisation of the industry, as traditional hand-
loom weavers were displaced by power looms. Thus as an ancillary development, the relatively specialist nature of the
spinning and weaving machinery dictated the establishment by
major textile firms of their own foundries.

Wars were a major source of prosperity for this industry. The
Crimean War of 1854-56 brought a demand for tents, sails and
soldiers' clothing, while demand for jute and linen during the
American Civil War was additionally stimulated by the non-
availability of cotton from the Southern States of America.
The earlier Crimean War had provided a further impetus to jute
manufacturers as there were fears regarding flax from Russia,
which supplied over 85% of Dundee's total flax imports (Warden,
1867, p.634). An additional source of demand for jute goods in
the 1850's was the opening up of Australia, with its large
British immigrant population, increased trade in primary
products and vast need for temporary canvas housing (Lenman,
Lythe and Gauldie, 1969, p.16); while an indication of the impact of later increases in demand may be seen in the fact that
the price of some goods rose by 50% in 1863 over their 1862
prices (Gauldie, 1969, pp.176-7). It is from this era that
some of the domestic architectural heritage of the textile
industry stems. So far as trade itself was concerned (Warden,
1867, Supplement p.14):

"The halcyon days which prevailed during the
latter part of the American war, and for some
time subsequent thereto, have left their mark
on the district. Old mills were rebuilt and
extended, and new ones erected; power-loom
factories sprung up in all directions, and for
a time builders and engineers had the entire
command of the position. The result has been
to transform and beautify and extend towns
previously prosperous, and to vivify and invig-
orate others which were fast falling into decay."

But the period culminating with the American Civil War was to
have an impact beyond the immediate prosperity which it
created. Not surprisingly, given the boom market, it was at
this time that backward vertical integration within the
industry began. The Cox firm established its own jute presses
near Calcutta in 1863; and in 1862 both Cox and Gilroy had
become shipowners. This period was also characterised by forward vertical integration as yarn spinners moved into the
weaving and finishing trades; and in retrospect this was also
seen to have been one of the greatest periods of technical
advance in the industry (Lenman, Lythe and Gauldie, 1969,
p.54). To the extent that the mid-century wars brought about
some over-expansion and collapse on the part of weaker firms,
they also contributed to a trend of concentration in the market and the recognition of the advantages of size and stability.
One of the benefits for the city's commerce as a whole stimulated by the textile boom was improved harbour facilities. The
Victoria Dock was opened in 1861, and the Camperdown Dock in
1864 (Carrie, 1953).

Set against this trend of expansion in Dundee, however, was
the gradual development of jute spinning and weaving in India
itself. This began in 1855, and it was only the war-time
demands of the mid 1850's to mid 1860's which delayed its impact upon the Dundee industry (Wallace, 1909). In fact the
Franco-Prussian war of the early 1870's provided only another
temporary military fillip to the industry which was by then
beginning to feel much more strongly the impact of the Calcutta
jute mills. Indeed Alexander Monfries noted that "a considerable period of wonderful prosperity" had come to an end by
1875; and "from being a paying business the making of jute
goods became a losing one and a good deal of machinery was
stopped. This was caused in great measure by the erection of
mills for the spinning of jute in Calcutta" (Gauldie, 1969,
pp.215-6). Calcutta goods were making serious inroads into
Dundee markets in America and Australia; and the Dundee industry

was finding it difficult to compensate for this in a Continental trade characterised by both the establishment of home jute
industries and increased protectionist tariffs. One area of
expansion for the Dundee industry, however, was the Scottish
linoleum trade based at Kirkcaldy. Nairn's of Kirkcaldy,
which dominated the Scottish market, was firmly established in
this field by the mid 1850's. It seems to be generally agreed,
nonetheless, that the jute trade was much less profitable from
the third quarter of the nineteenth century onwards; although
once again military conflict (the Boer War followed by the
South African War, and conflict between Russia and Japan in
1904-5) provided oases of prosperity.

THE EARLY TWENTIETH CENTURY

Lenman, Lythe and Gauldie paint a truly unhealthy picture of
the industry in the years leading up to 1914. Long-lived jute
barons who had made or inherited the fortunes of the 1850's and
1860's appeared unwilling to introduce much change into the
industry. These manufacturers, with interests in supplies of
raw jute and shipping services, and something of a monopoly of
business and social standing in the city, performed the function
of a barrier to new competition and new ideas in the industry.
Much of the "profit" in the industry, these authors (Lenman,
Lythe and Gauldie, 1969, pp.39-40) point out, came in fact
from judicious buying of raw jute, and manufacturing or processing costs were a small proportion of total. Indeed the peak of
capital investment in the jute industry appears to have occurred
in the late 1860's. Thereafter Dundee merchants seem to have
considered that the return on investment was greater on the other
side of the Atlantic (Jackson, 1968).

The hostilities of 1914-18 once again produced conditions of
high demand for the jute industry. By 1915 70% of the Dundee
industry's output was for Government Departments: it was boasted
that Dundee was producing one million sand bags per day at this
time. However, although World War I constituted a period of high,
if temporary, profits for the industry, it produced certain trends
which were to be of less long-term advantage to the industry as a
whole. War-time demand was a demand for coarse jute goods; and
the Dundee industry geared itself to this for the period, away
from the trend of the previous decades of counteracting competition from Calcutta by moving into finer jute goods markets. This
meant not only the use of existing plant in these "coarse"
markets, but also an element of "technical retrogression" as
possibilities for manufacturing improvements were ignored. Also
ignored were foreign markets; and this resulted in local
industries being established overseas to satisfy purely domestic

requirements. Not only were these markets protected by high
tariff barriers after 1918; in some cases they appear to have
exhibited a level of technology superior to that of Dundee
(Graham, 1928).

Because of problems of sea losses of raw material, and general
difficulties over supply, the industry had experienced some
fluctuations of fortune throughout World War I. But although
there was a temporary post-war boom in 1919-20 the remainder
of the decade witnessed a resumption of the earlier problems
of the industry. These centred around reduced overall demand
for jute, and continued competition in many markets from the
output of Calcutta mills. The Board of Trade Report of 1948
spoke (p.9) of the short-lived boom after 1918 being followed
by "tumbling prices and a declining demand", with unemployment
in the industry by the early 1930's exceeding 50%. The Dundee
jute industry was not even given much protection from imported
goods as India was exempted from the general round of import
duties imposed in 1932 by the operation of Imperial Preference.
In common with much of the remainder of British industry,
rationalisation occurred in an attempt to bring productive
capacity into line with reduced demand. In October 1920 a
number of established businesses were brought together to
form Jute Industries. A few years later, in 1924, a similar
arrangement resulted in the establishment of Low & Bonar; and
these two firms dominated the Dundee jute industry. These
amalgamations resulted in the two firms between them accounting
for over half of the Dundee jute trade (Jackson, J.M., 1979).

Thus although there were isolated areas of prosperity in the
industry in the immediate aftermath of World War I, the slump
of the late 1920's closed a large part of the industry. And
despite hopes that a slimmed-down industry characterised by
improved productivity and concentration upon the quality end
of the market would generate higher returns, this did not
materialise. In total, employment in the industry fell from
41,220 in 1924 to 27,980 in 1938: a fall of 32%. There was
an even more rapid decline in female employment over this
period - 39% - brought about by the use of new machinery
demanding more skilled male operatives. Another index of the
industry's declining fortunes was its diminished international
trading performance. At the end of the nineteenth century the
U.K. industry was exporting 75% of its output. This figure
never reached 20% in the 1930's; and in 1937 the industry for
the first time recorded an import surplus (Menzies and Chapman,
1946, p.246).

CONCLUSIONS ON THE EARLY HISTORY OF THE JUTE INDUSTRY

The Dundee jute industry, it is agreed, is one which can only
be fully understood in a historical context. The city had
already, by the early decades of the last century, become a
centre for linen manufacture - particularly of the coarse type
used for making cotton bagging and other forms of packaging.
The traditional flax industry progressed with mechanisation,
generally high demand for the product, and the operation of a
linen export bounty. But the continued need to search for
cheaper materials, the possibility of spinning jute on flax-
spinning machinery, the growing acceptability of jute by former
users of flax or hemp, the attractiveness of a raw material
(jute) which was free from the risk of interrupted supplies
dependent upon Britain's political relationship with Russia,
and, in time, the competition which flax bagging was beginning
to experience from Indian jute goods, all stimulated the foundation of a Dundee-based jute industry (Chapman, 1938 and 1939).

From this period on the industry expanded to a peak of prosperity in the early 1870's. The years of the Crimean War and
the American Civil War were of major significance in shaping
the industry, and Dundee raw jute imports rose from 16,590
tons in 1854 to 71,000 in 1865. This period saw the beginnings
of some of the major characteristics of the industry in the
twentieth century. Optimistic overtrading on the part of some
smaller firms, followed by financial collapse, emphasised the
value of size in an industry subject to cyclical sales booms
and slumps. The industry appears from this time to have become
more concentrated and more highly integrated. But what was in
more than one sense an Indian Summer for the Dundee jute trade
was coming to an end; and Lenman and Gauldie (1968) suggest
that the large orders of the Franco-Prussian War of 1870-73
represented the last period of easy profits. This is not to
say that the industry did not continue to grow. In 1873 Dundee
jute imports were 139,923 tons; a figure which expanded to
392,025 in 1895. Employment also expanded: from 14,911 persons
in 1870 to 43,360 in 1895. The jute industry also appears to
have continued its dominance of Dundee employment. The figure
for textile employment as a proportion of the total remained
at 48-49% in 1881 and 1911. In 1931 it was still 41%; and only
by 1951 had it fallen to 23% (Carstairs, 1968). The difficulties of the Dundee jute trade in the last decades of the nineteenth century were brought about by the very rapid expansion
of the Calcutta industry (to whom Dundee lost her Australasian
and South African markets and some of her American trade), and
the increased protectionist tariffs in Europe. For a time
Dundee was able to maintain a technological lead over Calcutta,

and to move ahead of that centre into finer jute goods.
Profitability may also have been maintained by continued concentration of the Dundee market into larger units, and the
decline in the general competitiveness of Dundee goods prior
to 1939 may have been disguised by the channelling of Government orders to Dundee rather than overseas, and stipulation of
the use of Dundee jute for some users such as beet sugar which
was Government subsidised.

The starting point of the main part of this study is thus the
demise of a traditional textile industry from its 19th century
heyday. It is a study, therefore, of how firms heavily committed to that industry reacted to continued overseas competition
and to new technologies such as paper bagging and containerisation. It involves an examination of how and why a relatively
small number of firms in a highly localised traditional market,
far away from many potential sources of demand for alternative
products, reacted to this situation and moved, with a creditable degree of success, into new market areas.

PROSPECTS FOR THE JUTE INDUSTRY IN 1945

The immediate background period of the major part of this
study commenced with the jute industry emerging from another
period of artificially stimulated demand, and with capacity
geared to the coarse end of the market. Once again the
industry appeared to be doomed to a consequent period of over-
capacity and further loss of neglected markets. As two
observers of the contemporary scene wrote (Menzies and Chapman,
1946, pp.260-1):

> "There is little doubt that, if the prospects of
> the jute industry seemed gloomy before the war
> (1939-45), they have become even more gloomy
> since. ... outside Europe as well as inside it,
> there is a very real danger that the war will
> have considerably speeded up India's encroach-
> ment on Dundee markets ... It seems also very
> probable that the war will again have stimulated
> the development of substitutes."

Some part of these gloomy prognostications was based upon a
phenomenon encountered by the industry immediately after 1918,
and which has already been referred to as "technical retrogression". During World War II Dundee had been very largely
geared towards providing basic jute goods for war-time needs.
This situation continued for some time after 1945 due, in the
first instance to Indian independence and Partition (see

below) which disrupted supplies of raw jute and basic jute
goods, and secondly to the outbreak of the Korean War in 1950
which again put the Dundee industry on a war footing. The
result of this was that Dundee lost further ground in those
specialist export markets which it had been trying to build
up prior to 1939: markets in which it avoided direct competition with the Calcutta mills. This problem was reinforced
by export quotas from the U.K. which applied until 1952. Thus
on the one hand Dundee was losing its place in world export
markets through quota restrictions, while on the other the
home industry was forced, as a result of the difficulties of
Partition, to expend most of its energies on production of
basic jute goods. For example, prior to 1947 India had
supplied two-thirds of U.K. cloth and bag requirements. With
the drying up of this source of supply three quarters of the
output of yarn from Dundee mills in the early 1950's was for
Hessians.

Not only was this the situation in Britain, but from the
early 1950's the Indian mills began a period of modernisation
and market reorientation which involved some of the owners
and managing agents in what has been referred to as "some
fairly ruthless rationalisation". Faced by considerable wage
increases, difficulties in obtaining certain supplies of raw
jute from East Pakistan, and the growth of jute industries in
other east Asian countries, the Calcutta mills installed
modernised spinning capacity and automatic weaving machines,
and moved into more sophisticated markets such as tufted
carpet backing for American customers, and also laminated
bags - a sandwich of jute and paper (Harrison, 1964).

Of even more immediate significance to the U.K. industry,
however, was the partition of the Indian subcontinent into
two independent states - India and Pakistan. The major
problem so far as jute was concerned was brought about by the
creation of a separate state of East Pakistan which had the
effect of dividing the jute growing area of Bengal (in East
Pakistan) from the merchanting and production centre around
Calcutta (in India). By this event 80% of the jute growing
area of Bengal was separated from India; and although economic relations between the two states were initially fairly
harmonious, trading and political differences arose which
culminated in Pakistan's failure to follow the British 30%
devaluation of 1949 while India did so. Restrictions on
supplies followed; and Britain was faced with a scarcity of
finished jute goods from Calcutta (because their mills lacked
raw jute from Bengal), and a reduced supply of raw jute from
Pakistan because of handling difficulties. These events,

combined with the increased demand occasioned by the Korean
war, not only quite obviously forced prices up and thereby
endangered jute's competitiveness with other materials, but
also meant that Dundee continued to produce basic jute goods
rather than diversify away from inevitable Indian competition.
The long term effect has been for Pakistan herself to develop
a jute manufacturing industry; and most of the jute goods
now imported to Dundee are from Pakistan - or Bangladesh as
it became in 1970. This latter country enjoys wage levels
lower than India and Bangladesh prices for jute goods may be
two-thirds those of India.

THE BOARD OF TRADE REPORT

In April 1946 a committee was constituted to look into the
operation of the U.K. jute industry. The committee's task,
in the words of its own terms of reference (Board of Trade,
1948), was as follows:

> "To examine and inquire into the various schemes
> and suggestions put forward for improvements of
> organisation, production and distribution methods
> and processes in the jute industry, and to report
> as to the steps which should be taken in the
> national interest to strengthen the industry and
> render it more stable and more capable of meeting
> competition in the home and foreign markets."

In general terms the Committee saw its job as being to
recommend the degree and form of protection appropriate to
safeguard the Dundee industry from competition from the Calcutta mills. The Committee saw protection as being necessary
in the light of the lower level of Indian wages; and it foresaw no other means of alleviating the growing incursion of
Indian goods into Dundee markets traditionally safe from such
competition. The Committee was thus aware that even in such
markets as quality sacking or in short runs of quality
Hessian, where Calcutta had previously not competed with
Dundee, there was a risk of the latter losing ground to the
former. Furthermore, although the Committee was to be concerned about the structure of the U.K. industry, it did not
feel that restructuring alone would offer adequate protection
from overseas competition. The Committee was thus sympathetic
to the need for some degree of general protection for the
home industry; and it felt that such protection had to be
applied to "standard lines" of jute goods, where there was
Indian competition, if the Dundee industry was to continue
on a healthy basis of producing both standard and quality

lines.

The quid pro quo, as it were, from the industry for this protection was to be re-equipment and reorganisation (i.e.
consolidation) on its part, so that long production runs could
be achieved, using modern spindles and looms efficiently laid
out, and which, the Committee evidently felt, could only be
afforded by more substantial enterprises. In other words, the
Committee saw it as being essential that the company consolid-
ations of the early 1920's, and the concentration of capacity
brought about by wartime exigencies should be continued.
Without such means the Committee foresaw a further contraction
of the industry, and a vicious circle of lost trade and competitiveness: "high costs, little if any profit, and no reserves
available for improvement and development" (Board of Trade,
1948, para.14). The Committee did not, however, view the
position of the Dundee industry as hopeless; and a number of
manufacturers were at the time of the Report installing new
machinery. Indeed paradoxically, in the light of the future
contraction of the industry, one of the Committee's worries
was over a potential labour shortage.

The acceptance of the feelings expressed in the Report gave
the Dundee jute industry a degree of protection - largely
operated through the continuance of Jute Control (see below) -
which undoubtedly slowed down its rate of decline. Although
the contingent amalgamations among producers did not take
place, it has been implied that the stability afforded by
Control did encourage modernisation of plant. For example,
between 1945 and 1951 an estimated £4 million was spent by the
industry on re-equipment (Times Publishing Co., 1952); and
this appears to have been a period of considerable modernisation in spinning and weaving, including improved plant layout
etc. Furthermore, although the system of protection may have
become of diminishing importance over time, the continuing
need to discuss the issue probably gave the industry an oligopolistic cohesion which may have militated against severe
competition among domestic producers. This is particularly
likely in view of the precise form in which Jute Control
"equated" or "marked up" prices of imported Indian goods: a
system which involved arriving at a consensus as to the
appropriate or fair price for Dundee goods. The Government-
sponsored system of protection through Control was also
accompanied by (or more questionably required the support of)
a series of restrictive trading agreements which were
practised by the industry until struck down by the Restrictive
Practices Court in 1963. The Report of the Jute Working Party
thus to a not inconsiderable extent contributed to the post-

war economic environment of the Dundee industry.

JUTE CONTROL

Some mention must be made of the function of Jute Control
because of the influence of this organisation on the post-war
industry. Technically it was a means of protecting the U.K.
industry from Indian competition. It may also, as mentioned
above, have served as a focal point for discussions about
pricing in the domestic market.

Originally Control was established in September 1939 and
covered raw jute, yarn, waste etc. In 1940 the regulations
were extended to imported jute goods; and although the policy
was originally designed to interfere as little as possible
with existing arrangements - and to operate through a system
of licences for existing merchants - Control eventually became
the sole importer of raw jute and jute goods in 1941 and 1942
respectively. Even so, Control still purchased through brokers
and shipping agents. A fairly comprehensive system of regulations was therefore established; and this included not only
licensing of spinners and weavers, but also licensing and
controls over the uses to which finished goods could be put.
Prices at each stage of the manufacturing process were also
laid down.

What distinguishes Control from other war-time regulations is
that the system was not wholly abandoned after hostilities
ceased. Certainly in September 1952 internal controls were
relaxed: i.e. the licensing and control of end-use of jute
goods were ended. Moreover in 1954 trading in raw jute was
returned to private hands. The Government of the day, on the
basis of the Board of Trade Report, nonetheless felt that in
respect of finished goods the Dundee industry required
continued protection. Jute Control thus continued to adjust
prices of imported jute goods so as to protect Dundee producers
from Indian competition. Imported goods were adjusted on the
basis of "equated prices" (by reference to the cost of raw
jute) or "markup prices" (by reference to landed prices of
imported jute goods). From 1954 to 1957 the system of
protection was largely based upon equated prices; but from
1957 onwards standard markups became the more common method,
until by 1963 this latter system accounted for 90% of Control
goods. The general trend over the years was towards a reduced
markup; and while the equated prices of the 1954-57 period
appear to have constituted a markup of some 47%, the formal
markup in July 1957 was set at 30%, and was reduced in January
1960 to 20%. Further reductions in the markup on some goods

and a return of others to free trade occurred during the early
1960's; and in May 1969 all imported goods previously subject
to Control were returned to private hands, although quotas
were retained in some cases.

MARKETS

With regard to end use markets, the jute industry in 1945 was
still dependent to a very large extent upon relatively unsophisticated uses of its output. Packaging was still the
major end use to which jute was put - accounting for about 70%
of total output of made-up jute according to one estimate
(Menzies and Chapman, 1946, p.253). This was to be of some
disadvantage to the Dundee industry. In the first place it
was an unstable market - dependent very much upon the volume
of domestic and international trade. This was a derived
demand which jute enjoyed only because of its cheapness.
Second, the packaging market for jute was the one in which it
was most susceptible to Indian competition, being a fairly unsophisticated product. Third, this was to be a market into
which new products such as paper and polythene, and new
methods such as containerisation, made considerable inroads on
the basis of efficiency and marketing appeal.

In its second most important market, however, - namely linoleum
backing - jute in 1945 enjoyed considerable advantages. The
greater special widths and higher quality demanded in this
market protected the Dundee industry from Calcutta. An
additional advantage in this sector was the nearness of the U.K.
linoleum manufacturing centre of Kirkcaldy in Fife. The disadvantage which Dundee was to encounter in this market was the
rapidly decreasing popularity of linoleum itself. Output
reached a peak annual output of 51.6m.sq. metres in 1955, and
thereafter rapidly declined to a corresponding figure of 8.9 in
1969 and to 4.0 in 1975.

Other uses of jute in the period after 1945 included carpeting,
cordage, and a number of minor uses such as cable insulation,
upholstery foundations, padding and stiffening of clothes, and
linings for boots and shoes.

An approximate idea of the total market situation around this
time may be gained from data provided in the Board of Trade
Working Party Report, although the figures relate to 1939 - the
last year when output was not influenced by the pre-war buildup of military requirements.

TABLE 1.2 U.K. Jute Production 1939 (tons)

Yarn: Carpet backing, twines,
            cordage etc.   50,150
            Jute carpets   3,050
            Webbing   600   53,800
                                                        ─────────
Cloth and Bags:

       Cloth: Hessian   28,200
               Sacking etc.   7,050   35,250
                                 ──────
       Bags   32,400   67,650
                                                        ─────────
                                                         121,450
                                                        ─────────

Source: Board of Trade (1948). Report of Jute Working
         Party. H.M.S.O., London. pp.17-19.

The same Report (p.19) went on to warn the Dundee Industry:

         "India had for many years supplied the home market
         for heavy bags made from low quality sacking and
         bagging; had made such heavy inroads in the
         hessian bag trade that there was every indication
         that as time went on the balance of that trade
         would gradually be lost to India; had made a
         start in the manufacture of linoleum hessian and
         brattice cloth; was encroaching more and more on
         the trade in other widths of hessian up to 72 ins.
         for non-bag uses; and was beginning to particip-
         ate in the trade in better quality sackings and
         tarpaulings. Thus virtually no normal home use
         for jute cloth and bags is likely to remain free
         from Indian competition in the future."

The years immediately after 1945 therefore saw the Dundee
jute industry as something of a watershed with regard to
markets for its output. There was no doubt that India was
poised to make further encroachments upon Dundee's traditional
markets, and that the total situation was likely to be aggravated by changes in technology such as containerisation and
the development of new forms of packaging.

         CONCLUSIONS

The purpose of the preceding sections of this chapter has
been to outline the state of the traditional jute industry in
1945 through both a brief economic history of the trade from
its origins to that date, and a summary of the condition of

the industry immediately after World War II.

In many ways this point in time represents a logical starting
date for any consideration of the industry up to the present.
Despite the industry being well past its major period of
growth, and in spite of the difficulties of the 1930's, the
trade, for some time largely unchanged in its economic structure or technology, looked forward with some hope to the post-
War world. However, major changes were about to occur over
the next 30 years - our period of study. Despite Government
and private efforts to modify the forces of import and
domestic competition, these were to increase significantly.
Domestic markets which at one time seemed large-scale and
relatively immune from the pressure of Asian competition were
to fall to technological and changes demand and import
competition. These forces brought about considerable restructuring of the traditional industry over the period from
the mid 1960's onwards. Finally, the industry was forced to
adopt quite radical technological and product market change
for its own survival into the 1970's. It is with an analysis
of these changes that the major part of this study is concerned.

References

Board of Trade (1948). Report of Jute Working Party.
H.M.S.O., London.

Carrie, D.C. (1953). Dundee and the American Civil War,
1961-65. Abertay Historical Society, Dundee. p.18.

Carstairs, A.M. (1968). The nature and diversification of
employment in Dundee in the twentieth century. In S. Jones
(Ed.), Dundee and District. British Association, London.
pp.320-28.

Carstairs, A.M. and A.V. Cole (1960). Recent developments
in the jute industry. Scot. Jour. of Pol. Econ., 7, 117.

Chapman, D. (1938). The establishment of the jute industry:
a problem for location theory. Rev. Econ. Stud., 6, 33-5.

Chapman, D. (1939). In R.L. Mackie (Ed.), Dundee and District.
British Association, London. pp.80-87.

Dean, P. (1965). The First Industrial Revolution. C.U.P.,
Cambridge. pp.84-9 and 121.

Gauldie, E. (1969). The Dundee Textile Industry 1790-1885.
Constable, Edinburgh.

Graham, D. (1928). The Dundee Jute Industry. Unpublished
Ph.D. Thesis, Dundee University. pp.125-7.

Harrison, G. (1964). <u>Bird and Company of Calcutta.</u> Bird & Co., Calcutta. pp.262-6 and 295-6.

Jackson, J.M. (1979). In J.M. Jackson (Ed.), <u>The Third Statistical Account of Scotland: The City of Dundee.</u> The Scottish Council of Social Service, Arbroath. p.121.

Jackson, W.T. (1968). <u>The Enterprising Scot.</u> Edinburgh University Press, Edinburgh. pp.21-4.

Lenman, B. and E. Gauldie (1968). The industrial history of the Dundee region from the eighteenth to the early twentieth century. In S. Jones (Ed.), <u>Dundee and District.</u> British Association, London. p.169.

Lenman, B., C. Lythe and E. Gauldie (1969). <u>Dundee and Its Textile Industry 1850-1914.</u> Abertay Historical Society, Dundee.

Menzies, I.E.P. and D. Chapman (1946). In H.A. Silverman (Ed.), <u>Studies in Industrial Organisation.</u> Methuen, London.

Rimmer, W.G. (1960). <u>Marshalls of Leeds: Flax Spinners, 1788-1886.</u> Cambridge University Press, Cambridge. Ch. 1.

Times Publishing Co. (1952). <u>Survey of United Kingdom Jute Industry.</u> Times Publishing Co., London. p.10.

Wallace, D.R. (1909). <u>The Romance of Jute: A Short History of the Calcutta Jute Mill Industry 1855-1909.</u> Empire Press, Calcutta.

Warden, A.J. (1867). <u>The Linen Trade, Ancient and Modern,</u> 2nd edition. Longmans Green, London.

Woodhouse, T. and A. Brand (1934). <u>A Century's Progress of Jute Manufacture, 1833-1933.</u> David Winter, Dundee. pp.15-16.

CHAPTER 2

ANALYSIS OF CHANGING MARKETS AND INDUSTRY STRUCTURE

INTRODUCTION

The purpose of this chapter is to trace the principal changes
in product markets in respect of what at the end of World War
II constituted the Dundee jute industry, and also to indicate
the major changes in industry structure. The material in this
chapter following the Introduction is divided into four
sections: analysis of changing markets, analysis of changing
market structure, analysis of other changes in market conditions, and a concluding section.

With regard to markets we want to know how the jute industry
and its constituent firms responded to the falling off of
demand from previous users. Some part of the answer to this
issue - indeed a major part - lies in diversification by former
jute manufacturers into other market areas altogether (analysed
in more detail in Chapter 3). Nonetheless, some part of this
chapter is devoted to examining changed market areas within the
jute industry itself, as well as to the movement by most firms
from dependence upon jute to a broader industrial textiles
base.

Changes in structure in a market, particularly a declining one,
are interesting in that they show us how the constituent firms
as a group reacted to external influences. Such changes may
also enable one to say something about the degree of competitiveness and efficiency in a market: a primary concern of
industrial economists. At the level of individual businesses,
it is also interesting to know how firms reacted to a sharp
falling off in demand for their principal traditional product.
Did firms move rapidly into other market areas; did they
simply go out of existence; or were they acquired by other

companies, either former competitors or firms based in other
markets?

In order to make some of the following data and analysis
easier to place in an overall context, a brief review is
first given of the transition of the jute industry during the
post-war period to 1977. This review identifies the major
trends and the principal forces at work; and it is in this
context that the remainder of the study should be placed.

The jute industry had undoubtedly benefited from the 1939-45
war so far as stimulation of demand was concerned. Indeed,
according to a number of people in the trade today looking
back, it was only the enormous sandbag contracts of 1938 onwards which enabled the industry to survive the 1930's. These
contracts were costed at local conversion rates ("real Dundee
prices", as one industrialist put it), and thus ushered in a
period during which the local industry was freed from the full
impact of Asian competition.

The Dundee industry emerged from World War II under the protection of Jute Control (outlined in the previous chapter);
and this system, combined with the trade pricing agreements
operated by the industry itself, not only protected the
domestic industry from import competition, but also militated
against the emergence of domestic rivalry. The late 1940's
and the early 1950's were a period of adjustment for the
Dundee industry. Manufacturing premises were gradually
returned to the trade from war-time use following concentration. Caird's Ashton Works and James Scott's Mid Wynd Works
had, for example, been used for light engineering and jerrican
manufacture. Jute output at this time was experiencing consistent demand for yarn for woven carpets, and backing cloth
for linoleum. In both of these areas the Dundee trade had a
technical and transport cost advantage over India; and as
will be seen in the main body of this chapter, a high proportion of the output of the Dundee industry went into floorcoverings. By the mid 1950's however, changes were taking
place in these markets. The system of import protection had
started to price jute bags out of competition with multiwall
paper bags. The latter were being developed by the major
paper manufacturers such as Reed and Bowater; and as part of
their marketing strategy these latter firms also produced
bag-filling plant. From this time on, therefore, the markets
for transporting animal feeds etc. were lost by jute to paper
bags, while grain, and in time other products, became subject
to bulk handling. At this time too the linoleum market began
its downward trend towards eventual near extinction, and the
total situation was one of potential severe loss for the

traditional jute industry.

The situation was saved by the advent, in Georgia in the
United States, of a tufted carpet industry. Although the
backing market for this product looked at one time as if it
might be served by cotton, jute proved to have superior technical characteristics, and became adopted for both primary
and secondary tufted carpet backing. This situation was
particularly fortuitous. Only in the early 1950's had U.K.
export quotas been relaxed; and the tufted carpet backing
market was originally an export one as the U.K. and European
public continued to prefer traditional woven carpets. Furthermore tufted carpet backing could be woven on existing jute
looms used to produce linoleum backing. Only limited improv-
isation and re-equipment was therefore necessary to accommo-
date minor modifications: for example, twill rather than plain
weave was required. In addition, the technical requirements
(75% of the backing was 4yd. width and a further 15% 5yd.)
limited, at least for a time, Asian competition; while transport distances for Indian and Dundee firms were about the same
to American markets. Thus the tufted carpet backing market in
the late 1950's and the early 1960's was an enormous boon to
the U.K. jute industry. For although the U.S. and Canadian
markets were eventually lost to Asian competition, the early
1960's saw the beginnings and rapid expansion of a U.K. and
European tufted carpet industry. Here was a source of rapidly-
expanding demand for jute on Dundee's doorstep, relatively
speaking; and the rate of expansion of the market gave the
Dundee industry for a time something which it had not experienced for almost a century - a sellers market in jute cloth.
On this basis the early 1960's witnessed considerable re-
equipment in the industry - for example with twill weave looms.

The final phase of development covered by this study witnessed,
however, the almost total disappearance of the local jute
industry on any scale. The cause of this was a man-made fibre -
polypropylene - which could be woven into a cloth. It took
over from jute both as a carpet backing material and also in
container manufacture. Jute's periodical shortage of supply
and unpredictability of price caused it to be ousted by what
is essentially a by-product of petroleum refining. The tufted
carpet industry in particular took up polypropylene in place
of jute on price grounds; and most of the original jute manufacturers have now turned to polypropylene weaving, with some
of the larger companies having also established facilities for
extruding the polypropylene tape from the chemical chips or
granules. Labour usage in particular has declined in the
industry as the new looms for weaving polypropylene operate
at something like twice the speed of the former jute looms,

and can be supervised on the basis of one person for every
five or six modern Sulzer looms compared with one person for
every two or three jute looms. For example in one of McDowall's studies (McDowall and Draper, 1978, p.8) it was pointed
out that a given square yardage of polypropylene woven on the
most modern looms required only one sixth of the labour of the
same area of jute woven on traditional looms. This represents
a reduction of 83% in labour usage.

Over the period since the late 1960's, therefore, the former
Dundee jute industry has been transformed into a broader
industrial textiles one; and Dundee itself has become a
centre of some importance in the new field, with an estimated
two-thirds of polypropylene production being carried on in the
Dundee and Forfar area. Thus, as mentioned before, this study
is one of transition as much as one of decline. As the
summary figures below indicate, nonetheless, the history is at
least to begin with one of decline. The purpose of this
chapter is now to indicate in more detail the changes in
product markets and market structure associated with that
decline.

TABLE 2.1 U.K. Jute Industry

| | Output ('000 tonnes) | | Employment* | Number of |
	yarn	cloth	('000)	Firms**
1948	101.9	59.9	20.3	37
1956	144.5	90.1	19.1	39
1960	144.1	83.5	17.2	32
1966	122.8	73.1	17.1	30
1967	113.8	64.6	15.3	30
1968	111.5	59.7	15.2	29
1969	107.9	52.7	15.4	29
1970	87.5	40.9	11.9	25
1971	77.6	32.0	10.3	21
1972	74.7	26.5	9.4	16
1973	68.2	24.2	9.0	16
1974	57.5	20.9	9.4	16
1975	51.1	16.3	8.1	16
1976	52.7	16.1	8.1	15
1977	46.8	13.8	8.0	14

*   employees in employment
** full members of the Association of Jute Spinners &
    Manufacturers.

Sources: output - <u>Annual Abstract of Statistics</u>. H.M.S.O.,
         London.
         employment - <u>British Labour Statistics</u>. H.M.S.O.,

London.

firms - Association of Jute Spinners & Manufacturers.

ANALYSIS OF CHANGING MARKETS

The history of changing markets in the context of this
industry is essentially that of firms trying to find new uses
for jute to replace the loss of traditional floorcovering outlets, and of the same firms going over to the manufacture of
synthetic fibres - especially polypropylene. Difficulties
arise in statistical analysis in this area because much of
the yarn output of jute manufacturers is used by those firms
to make jute cloth - i.e. a large proportion of the firms are
vertically integrated. There may thus be a danger of "double
counting" here in allocating output to various market areas.
Many statistics are fairly aggregated; and one study was only
able to suggest that half of the yarn output of the industry
went into bags and floorcoverings/furnishings (Jackson, 1979,
pp.113-4).

What does appear to be the case, however, is that many of the
Dundee firms in the years immediately after 1945 became
heavily committed to supplying the floorcoverings market, and
that their fortunes became inextricably linked to the pattern
of cyclical demand for floorcoverings in general, and to
changes in technology or fashion as linoleum gave way to woven
and subsequently tufted carpets, and more recently to tiles.
Caird (Dundee) is one particular instance of a firm which became heavily orientated to the linoleum industry in the early
1950's; and this affected the firm's subsequent pattern of
diversification (see Chapter 3). But other firms were often
only slightly less so committed. William Halley & Sons, for
example, sold 75% of their yarn and cloth output in the early
1960's to the floorcovering industry (Dundee Chamber, June
1961, p.860); and the corresponding figure for Jute Industries - the largest firm in the market - was 60% (Financial
Times, 16.2.60). For the market as a whole an estimate in
the late 1950's put the proportion at around 50%.

The disappearance of traditional markets

The first major change with which the industry had to contend
was the rapid falling off in demand for linoleum from the
early 1960's. Output of linoleum built up after 1945 to an
annual peak of 51.6m.sq.m. in 1955, and remained on a high
plateau until the end of the decade. From then, however,
demand fell off very rapidly: from 47.8m.sq.m. in 1960 to
30.9 by 1963 and 11.2 by 1968. By 1977 the figure had fallen

to 3.6m.sq.m. per annum. In addition to this falling off in
total linoleum sales there was a trend as early as the 1950's
towards linoleum being backed with bitumenised paper in place
of hessian. There was nothing which jute manufacturers could
do in the face of the loss of this source of derived demand
as consumers moved to soft floorcoverings. But the loss was
keenly felt by the Dundee industry as it was a market area in
which competition from India and Pakistan had been held at
bay by the high quality and modern technology offered by the
Dundee trade.

Another major change which was to have a serious effect upon
the jute industry was the growth of new methods in the bulk
handling of primary commodities. This was a market in which
jute had established a powerful position by virtue of the
cheapness of the material (including the reusable nature of
the ubiquitous jute bag), and its ability to "breathe", while
also for some purposes being capable of being made proof
against mildew or water. The bulk handling of commodities
such as wheat, maize, flour and sugar obviously became much
more attractive relative to bagging in those economies where
crops were grown on a large scale, where considerable transporting distances were involved, or where labour was expensive. Although some economies had begun bulk handling of
crops prior to 1939, this process rapidly gained momentum in
less developed countries during the 1950's; and the newer
concept of containerisation of the 1960's further ate into
market areas where jute sacking and packaging had once pre-
dominated. Other minor areas of jute usage which have now
been transferred to other materials are twines, road haulage
and building site tarpaulins, furnishings, cargo separators
and, of course, jute carpets. The loss of these areas to
more sophisticated products such as P.V.C. added to the
problems of jute's loss of its major end-use markets.

It is also worth mentioning at this stage that jute has not
always been competitive with other traditional fibres on a
price basis; and that frequent price fluctuations and political uncertainty have further diminished the attractiveness
of jute in some market areas. Thus, although cotton bags do
not normally compete with jute, high prices for the latter
or a glut of the former crop have produced times when cotton
was preferred: for example in the early 1950's. A more
serious problem for manufacturers and users of jute products
has been the tendency for raw jute prices to fluctuate
rapidly, depending upon crop conditions and the political
climate in India and Pakistan. This is initially, of course,
a problem for spinners and weavers of jute, who go "long" or
"short" on raw material depending upon expectations of future

price movements. Thus the chairman of Thomson Shepherd commented in the mid 1950's that "raw jute supplies and prices
over the past year have, as usual, been a matter of constant
anxiety" (Thomson Shepherd & Co., 1956 Annual Report); and
one manufacturer was quoted as saying "you can be technically
as efficient as you like, but you lose money if you buy (raw
jute) at the wrong time" (Financial Times, 14.12.64). With
raw jute accounting for about 50% of total costs, this is
obviously an area of concern to management. It has even been
suggested to the author by someone of experience in the
industry that one firm at least has survived in the market by
buying raw jute (either for stockholding in Dundee, or simply
"buying forward") and selling it at an advantageous price to
competitor manufacturers. This uncertainty with regard to
prices may have fed through to some jute goods users and
hastened their adoption of a commodity with a more stable
pattern of prices.

The growth of polypropylene

Undoubtedly the major change in the jute industry over the
past two decades has been the growth in this country,
following their popularity in the United States, of a market
for tufted carpet floorcoverings. In 1957, the first year in
respect of which data are available, tufted carpets accounted
for about 7% of U.K. carpet output by area. But from an
annual output figure of 3.3m.sq.m. in that year, output of
tufted carpets rose to 27.8m.sq.m. in 1964 and to 89.7 m.sq.m.
in 1972. The 1977 output figure of 123.4m.sq.m. meant that
tufted carpets by then accounted for 73% of U.K. carpet output by area - a proportion which had grown from 59% as late
as 1972. These data are of some importance not only in indicating the extent of a market from which jute initially
benefited, but also in highlighting a major market area where
polypropylene has been substituted for jute. The latter was
used for wefts and for stuffer warp in woven carpets (the
main warp being traditionally made of cotton), and for both
primary and secondary backing of tufted carpets. Polypropylene's first use was as primary backing on tufted carpets;
but from there its use in floorcoverings has expanded to
woven carpet wefts and also of course to producing carpet
pile or face yarns.

Polypropylene has also taken the place of jute in other market
areas; and this began happening to such an extent in the
late 1960's that many of the traditional jute manufacturers
moved significantly into polypropylene at that time. Such a
dominant feature of the local industry has this been that the
local business journal commented of the emergence of polypro-

pylene that "no other development in the long history of the
jute industry has made such an impact" (Dundee Chamber, Dec.
1971, p.639). Because of the importance of the coming of
polypropylene onto the local scene the product deserves a
brief technical and economic introduction before taking the
market analysis further.

Polypropylene is a synthetic fibre as opposed to the general
class of natural (vegetable or animal) fibres. It derives
from a class of macro-molecular materials called polymers,
which are known to be built up from simple chemical units,
monomers. From the class of polymers referred to as linear
(long and thin) chemists realised they could form fibres.
Because polypropylene solution is made from a manufacturer
material (as opposed to those man-made fibres which, like
viscose or rayon, contain a natural product and are therefore
referred to as "regenerated") it is known strictly as a
synthetic. Other synthetic fibres include Nylon, Terylene
and Orlon.

The class of synthetic fibres from which polypropylene derives is known as polyolefins; and of these only polyethylene
(polythene) had by the late 1950's achieved commercial success.
Polypropylene was therefore responsible for the commercial
growth of the polyolefin class from that time; and it owed
its original success to the cheapness of its raw material -
propylene - available in very large quantities from the
petroleum industry (Hossack, 1968). Polymerised propylene
can be melted, extruded and slit into tape form, the tape
then being wound on to a spool ready for weaving. The cheapness of the raw material and the contour of the tape contributed to its success in yarn and woven form in competition
with jute after the first commercial production of tape in
the early 1960's; and jute from this period onwards began
to suffer from competition in the carpet backing and bag
markets - the latter also being competed for by high and low
density polyethylene.

With regard to the general economics of polypropylene production, the major contrast with jute lies in the capital-
intensive nature of the total manufacturing process from the
petroleum feedstock onwards. One estimate suggests that of
total manufacturing costs of polypropylene, capital investment represents 35% of the total as opposed to 26% for the
basic feedstock, and 27% for power etc. This implies quite
clearly that, unlike the jute industry, polypropylene manufacturing profitability is very sensitive to activity levels,
and that raw material price changes have a reduced impact
upon total production costs. The other point about polypro-

pylene production is that costs have been generally declining
since the mid 1960's. In the U.K., for example, the list
price of polypropylene resin fell by 38% in money terms in
the decade to 1972; and, as emphasised in more detail below,
there have been other factors exerting a downward pressure
upon polypropylene prices (Grilli, 1975, pp.65-9).

With regard to its market impact, polypropylene use advanced
particularly with the adoption of tufted carpets in this
country, although latterly the fibre has also been used for
woven carpet backing. The rapidity with which the former use
of polypropylene took place may be gauged from the fact that
its use for the primary backing of tufted carpets rose from
less than 10% in 1967 to some 95% in 1974 (McDowall, Draper
and McGuinness, 1976, pp.47-8). Not only has jute suffered
in some of the more sophisticated markets from the use of
polypropylene as a substitute, but even in traditional
packaging areas the new fibre may have more marketing appeal,
or simply be more efficient. For example, it was reported
that in the late 1960's the Australian wool trade was moving
from the use of traditional jute wool packs to polypropylene:
raising usage of the latter from 400,000 in 1968 to 1,500,000
in 1969 (Financial Times, 9.4.69). Natural hard fibres such
as sisal used for twines and other cordage have also become
vulnerable to competition from polypropylene as prices of
these have risen steeply. McDowall, Draper and McGuinness
estimate that for Western Europe as a whole the use of polypropylene for bags and industrial cloth rose from 2,500 metric tons in 1967 to 61,000 metric tons in 1974, and that by
the latter date 45% of all sacks produced in the U.K. were
made from polypropylene (McDowall, Draper and McGuinness,
1976, p.48). So far as competition for jute is concerned,
further inroads into this last market have also been made by
high-density polyethylene. The basic factors considered in
choosing jute packaging are not only the relative price of
jute vis-a-vis, say, multi-wall paper bags or products of
the polyolefin class, but also characteristics such as
ability to "breathe" or to put up with rough handling or to
be reusable (all of which jute possesses). In those market
areas, for example fertilizers, where reuse is uncommon,
where presentation of the packaged commodity is important,
or where the packaged product is hygroscopic - i.e. where it
has the capacity to absorb water from the air and where this
leads to a deterioration in the product's condition - other
forms of packaging are competitive. It should be emphasised
in this context that the adoption of polypropylene for carpet
backing required considerable efforts on the part of producers to eliminate technical problems involved in polypropylene's
use in this area. Not only did difficulties arise initially

in cutting the woven polypropylene without producing fraying
and thus waste of material, but there was also initially a
problem of dimensional stability. Further problems encountered in the tufted carpet industry were those of poor bonding
between the latex used to lock the face pile tufts into the
primary backing and the polypropylene itself, and the shrink-
age of the polypropylene backing during the curing or drying
of the rubber latex: up to 20% initially. Finally, polypropylene does not easily accept dyes, and this can produce "grin"
as the natural colour of the backing shows through the
colours of the surface pile. This last problem was overcome
by needling nylon into the primary backing - a fibre which
can easily be dyed. Thus in technical terms polypropylene has
only come to compete with jute as a result of considerable
investments of effort and money (see Gay and Jenkins, 1970;
Overton, 1969).

With regard to the question of price competition between jute
and synthetic substitutes, the first point to note is that
bag making and carpet backing do not constitute a large part
of total usage of polypropylene or polyethylene. Increases
in demand from these areas are thus unlikely to have a major
impact upon price. That is, in comparison with jute, the use
of polypropylene in its place is characterised by a highly
price elastic supply. Furthermore, during the mid 1960's
when polypropylene was first being marketed commercially in
this context, it was felt that further technical advances,
the achievement of production economies of scale together
with beneficial "learning" effects, and general competitive
pressures would produce a situation such that, relative to
prices in general, the cost would fall. That this expectation
was borne out may be seen from the fact that over the period
1959-1965 the price of polypropylene fell from 45 pence per
lb. to 24 pence per lb., while that of high density polythene
fell over the same period from 42 to 21 pence per lb. (Financial Times, 11.6.66). The comparative situation is emphasised
in a World Bank survey which compared selling prices of raw
jute and polypropylene polymer. Taking 1962 as 100 in each
case, the 1975 index for polypropylene was 73 (and it had
fallen as low as 46 in 1970), while that for jute had climbed
steadily over the period to 163 in 1975 (Grilli, 1974, p.43).
Furthermore, with regard to the impact of oil price increases
on polypropylene, one has to bear in mind that the effect of
such price rises will be diluted as one moves along the manufacturing and selling chain from feedstock to final product.
One estimate suggests that a 100% increase in oil prices
might lead to a 10%-15% increase in that of a polymer product
such as polypropylene film (Grayling, 1975). What also has
to be re-emphasised in the price context is that polypropylene

production is characterised by a high ratio of fixed to
variable costs. This not only offers considerable scope for
production economies; but also means that raw material cost
increases have a reduced impact upon final product prices
compared with the case of jute where the raw material traditionally comprises around 50% of total costs. Finally, it may
be noted that although the market supplying the basic polypropylene polymer is oligopolistic, the pressure of competition
and the balance between supply and demand in recent years have
meant that raw material price increases have frequently been
absorbed by petrochemical manufacturers rather than passed on
to feedstock users.

Finally in this section, it would have been useful to have
been able to trace the changing composition of jute industry
output by reference to different end uses. This would have
indicated clearly the decline of various jute end-use markets
and the reaction to this on the part of manufacturers in terms
of moving into other areas. Unfortunately such data over the
period of this study are scarce and unsatisfactory. One of
the firms in the industry, Scott & Robertson, has published
in its Annual Report a breakdown of end-use markets. These
indicate the cyclical upward trend in floorcovering uses, a
roughly similar pattern in agriculture, and a falling off
under the headings of Building, Chemicals, and Food. This
end-use analysis, however, refers to the total product output
of the firm - both jute and synthetics - and is thus of little
value in tracing developments in jute alone when the proport-
ions of jute and synthetics output were themselves changing
significantly over the period. Only one reliable and relevant source in the area of end uses of jute appears to exist,
and is reproduced below in Table 2.2.

The most obvious feature of the data in Table 2.2 is the
absolute and proportional reduction in the importance of
packaging and sacking end uses for jute over the period.
This trend applies to carpet backing cloth in absolute terms.
Output in the U.K. in respect of the first three output
classes in Table 2.2 declined by 54%, 52% and 28% over the
period.

TABLE 2.2   United Kingdom: Estimated Consumption of Jute
and Jute Goods by Major End Uses

	1965		1968		1970		1971	
	'000 tonnes	%	'000 tonnes	%	'000 tonnes	%	'000 tonnes	%
Bags and sacks	35.0	21	31.0	20	20.0	17	16.0	15
Other packaging, industrial etc. uses	52.0	31	44.0	28	36.0	30	25.0	23
Carpet backing cloth	23.0	14	26.5	17	18.0	15	16.5	15
Carpet yarn	48.5	29	45.8	29	38.0	32	42.0	39
Cordage, cable etc.	5.0	3	5.0	3	4.0	3	3.5	3
Felts and padding	4.0	2	4.0	3	4.0	3	4.0	4
	167.5	100	156.3	100	120.0	100	107.0	99*

* due to rounding.

Source: Grilli, E.R. and others (1974). Jute and Synthetics,
I.B.R.D. Staff Working Paper, No. 171, 1974, Annex II,
p.35.

ANALYSIS OF MARKET STRUCTURE

Market structure is analysed here because of its importance in
determining the conduct or behaviour and performance of the
industry, and because changes in the structure of the industry
are also the outcome of fundamental changes in the market.

With regard to the statistics, it should be emphasised in
dealing with market structure below that the data are used to
analyse the changes in market structure as a whole in the
industry over the period studied, and are not designed to
measure market concentration alone - although the latter is,
of course, of considerable interest. It is for this reason,
and also because none of the sources of information is itself
entirely satisfactory, that a range of types of data has been
used.

Broad changes in industry structure

With regard to aggregated data, Census of Production figures
can be used to give a very broad idea of the most important
changes in the structure of the jute industry on an enterprise
basis since 1958. The most unfortunate aspect of this data is
the changes in the basis and classification of the material

over the period, and this leads to a lack of full comparability between sets of figures.

TABLE 2.3 Jute Industry Enterprise Distribution by Employment

Numbers Employed	Enterprises								
	1958*	1963*	1968	1970	1972	1973	1975	1976	1977
1- 99	18	5	25	22	19	23	22	24	24
100- 199	9	10	10	9	8	10	10	7	8
200- 299	6	4	11	9	7***	7	5	5	3
300- 399	6	3	4	6**	3	3***	6**	4***	4***
400- 749	6	5	5	-	‾**	‾**	-	‾**	‾**
750-4,999	3	5		-	4**	4**	-	3**	3**
	48	32	55	46	41	47	43	43	42
	(64)	(44)	(43)	(43)	(35)	(38)	(40)	(39)	(37)

*   firms employing 25 or more persons
**   300+
***   300-499
**** 500+

Note: The figures in brackets for each year represent in all
       cases the total number of enterprises in the industry.
       The figures immediately above are larger for 1968-1977
       because enterprises may classify themselves in more than
       one size group on the basis of having establishments in
       more than one size group.

Sources: Board of Trade/Department of Industry, Census of
         Production, 1958, Part 80; 1963, Part 79; 1968,
         Part 102; 1970, Part C102; 1972-77, Business
         Monitor PA415.

Enterprise data enable us to say something about the economic
power structure in the industry. In general those in Table 2.3
above indicate, within their limits, the reduction in numbers
among the small and medium sized firms, and the possible
growing dominance of the industry by the largest firms.

What one would ideally wish to measure on the basis of Census
data is the degree of homogeneity (low variance or standard
deviation) of firm size or log of firm size, and so more even
distribution of market shares or otherwise. Industries becoming
more concentrated would thus tend to be characterised by a
rising standard deviation of the distribution of firm sizes.
Unfortunately the Census of Production data above do not lend
themselves to this analysis because of the changing size classes
over the period of analysis, and the open-ended nature of the

top size class.

Given the relatively unsatisfactory nature of the Census data,
further investigation using trade statistics was carried out.
With regard to size distribution and concentration figures
there are two pieces of data. The first of these merely enables us to confirm the market concentration which was taking
place in the industry from 1945 until the early 1960's. Further data provided by the international trade association,
however, allows us to take the analysis somewhat further over
the more recent period.

At the time of the industry's defence of its restrictive
trading agreements before the Restrictive Practices Court in
1962 it was pointed out that over the period 1947 to 1962 the
number of spinning firms in the industry had fallen from 26
to 18, and that of weavers from 36 to 24. In respect of
market concentration, it was shown on the same occasion that
the proportion of raw jute consumed by the 7 largest spinners
had risen from 63.8% to 70.7% over the period; and in weaving
the proportion of looms owned by the 7 largest weavers had
risen over the same period from 49.3% to 58.6%. What is also
revealed by the data at this time is the continued dominance
of the industry by Jute Industries. This was still by far the
largest firm in 1962 with an estimated 5,500-6,000 employees;
and was only followed at some distance by a group of five or
six firms, each employing 750-1,500 persons (Robertson, 1962,
pp.4 and 39-40).

More detailed figures are available for a later period only,
and these reveal the following situation.

TABLE 2.4   U.K. Jute Industry: Size Distribution of Firms by
            Employment

	Size					
	-50	51-100	101-500	501-1,000	1,0001+	Total
1957	2	9	23	5	3	42
1958	2	12	16	5	2	37
1959	2	12	16	5	2	37
1960	2	10	15	5	2	34
1961	3	9	15	5	2	34
1962	2	8	15	5	2	32
1963	2	6	16	5	2	31
1964	2	7	15	5	2	31
1965	2	6	15	4	2	29
1966	2	6	14	4	2	28
1967	2	6	14	4	2	28
1968	2	6	14	4	2	28
1969	2	4	14	4	2	26
1970	2	3	13	4	2	24
1971	2	2	11	3	2	20
1972	1	2	11	3	2	19
1973	1	2	11	3	2	19
1974	1	2	10	3	2	18
1975	1	2	8	3	2	16
1976	1	2	7	2	3	15
1977	1	2	6	2	3	14

Data refer to members of the Association of Jute Spinners and
Manufacturers.

Differences between the Total column of this Table and that
in Table 2.5 may be accounted for by the timing and definition
bases of the two sets of data which are from different sources.

Source: Association of European Jute Industries Statistical
        Yearbook. A.E.J.I., Paris.

Unfortunately even these data are not perfect. There appears
in particular to be some confusion over the identity of the
firms in the 1,001+ employment range. From 1968 to 1977
(1968 was the first year for which individual company employment data were revealed in company Annual Reports) four firms
would appear to qualify for inclusion in this category: Sidlaw,
Low & Bonar, Scott & Robertson, and Don Bros. Buist. Low &
Bonar may have been excluded on the grounds that jute was only
a small part of its total output (around 10% in the mid 1960's
according to a senior executive), although the company was a
member of the A.J.S.M. until 1975, and had an estimated 10-15%
of the industry's output in the mid 1960's.

What the data in Table 2.4 nonetheless illustrate is not only
the dominance of this particular industry by a small group of
relatively large firms, but also the way in which the industry
was restructured and the impact upon different size classes of
firms of the decline of the traditional market for jute. Most
obviously the middle size classes of firms appear to have been
worst affected by the market decline. Those firms which in
1957 had 51-500 employees suffered by far the greatest drop in
their number - and in the case of those in the 101-500 employees group the drop was particularly rapid during the time of the
industry's transition to polypropylene after the late 1960's.

Relating purely to the number of firms in the industry, we have
data on membership of the jute trade association from 1945 to
1977. Membership of the Association of Jute Spinners and Manufacturers is not comprehensive so far as the trade is concerned.
Nonetheless it was estimated that in 1962 membership covered
100% of spinning capacity (apart from two small English spinners) and 90% of loomage (Robertson, 1962, p.19). The data in
Table 2.5 below refer to full (as opposed to associate) membership of the Association. This is felt to be more appropriate,
as associate members include textile machinery manufacturers;
but it has had the effect of eliminating a few local firms
which were acquired by larger concerns in the 1960's, and thus
understates both the rate of contraction of the industry and
also the extent of acquisition by larger firms of smaller competitors.

TABLE 2.5   Full Members of the Association of Jute Spinners
            & Manufacturers

1945	39	1956	40	1967	30
1946	39	1957	40	1968	29
1947	39	1958	40	1969	29
1948	37	1959	38	1970	25
1949	38	1960	33	1971	21
1950	38	1961	33	1972	16
1951	38	1962	31	1973	16
1952	40	1963	30	1974	16
1953	40	1964	30	1975	16
1954	40	1965	30	1976	15
1955	40	1966	30	1977	14

* Data as at February of each year.

Source: A.J.S.M., Association Yearbook.

The figures above confirm our picture of an industry whose
decline set in during the mid 1960's and accelerated by the
early 1970's. Apart from a sudden increase in the number of

disappearances in 1959, when three firms were acquired by
other members of the industry and two simply went out of
business, the number of independent firms fell quite steadily
by almost 25% from 1945 to 1967. From this latter date onwards, however, the number of firms halved in a decade. It
is thus during this latter period that there has been the
greatest adjustment. Some of the reduction in Association
membership over this period reflects continuing or surviving
firms leaving the jute industry. Low & Bonar, Caird, and
Thomson Shepherd all fall into this category. Ignoring for a
moment the merger of Unijute and James Scott, dealt with
below, this leaves a total of twelve firms which actually
went out of independent existence between 1967 and 1977. Of
these firms seven were family businesses which ceased to exist
due to a combination of the impact of the rapid falling off in
demand in the industry and the absence of family succession.
The remaining five were acquired by other larger firms within
the industry, with no single firm playing a dominant role in
this process.

Mergers and acquisitions

There are broadly two types of change which are responsible
for movements in market structure over time: these are
"deaths" and "acquisitions". The former occur as firms cease
manufacture; the latter are brought about by takeover. It is
not always possible, however, to distinguish clearly between
these two, as some businesses may be acquired and rapidly
closed down by the new parent. In this case what appears to
have been an acquisition may in reality have been a death.

The contraction of the jute industry has produced not only
significant mergers but also acquisitions of smaller businesses by the larger existing firms in the market, as well as a
number of deaths or disappearances by minor companies. Undoubtedly the major amalgamation of the period was the merger
between Robertson Industrial Textiles (which traded as Unijute)
and The Mid Wynd Holding Co. (whose two principal operating
subsidiaries were James Scott & Sons and Thomas Boag & Co.).
This merger took place in April 1965; and although Scott and
Boag were the dominant concerns, with a joint capital of
£1,363,047 in contrast to Robertson's £552,989, the joint
group became known as Scott & Robertson (Financial Times,
1.4.65). It has been estimated that a few years earlier the
Mid Wynd Holding Co. was the second largest spinner and
weaver of jute in the U.K. (Jackson, 1979, p.126); and by
the time of the presentation of the first set of combined asset
figures for Scott & Robertson the total assets were in excess
of £5m. compared with Jute Industries' £6.5m. These asset

figures, however, may overstate the market position of Scott
& Robertson relative to Jute Industries. Employment data
indicate a greater dominance by Jute Industries; and estimates within the trade suggest that by the mid-to-late 1960's
Jute Industries still had some 45% of jute sales as against
just over 20% for Scott & Robertson. Nonetheless, this type
of merger, and the growth of such firms as Caird (Dundee),
H. & A. Scott and others in the middle size range, meant that
the very largest businesses were beginning to lose some part
of their earlier hegemony, particularly as some of the giants
in the industry - notably Low & Bonar - were becoming less
solely committed to the jute industry.

The 1960's was also a time during which the larger spinners
and manufacturers were buying up smaller firms. By some
people in the industry this has been explained in terms of a
shortage of good labour, and therefore the quest to find a
suitable workforce rather than additional plant. There is no
doubt, however, from the way in which these acquisitions have
been subsequently "rationalised" or simply closed down that a
process of takeover of small firms and their subsequent closure was felt to be a more "orderly" method by which the
industry as a whole could contract its capacity into line with
falling demand. The alternative might have been the continued
existence of small mills and factories, offering goods at
minimal prices on the basis of assets already fully depreciated,
and forcing similar price concessions on the part of other
firms. Sidlaw Industries, for example, acquired a number of
smaller spinning and weaving enterprises over the period from
the late 1950's to the mid 1960's, including D. & R. Duke of
Brechin, John Lowson of Forfar, Alex Henderson & Sons, Tayport
Spinning Co., and more recently South Mills (Textiles) in
Dundee. Also into this category of adjustment fall James
Scott's earlier acquisition of Mitchell Cotts, Caird's purchase
of Alex Moncur and J. & D. Wilkie's acquisition of fellow
Kirriemuir spinner Ogilvie Bros. in 1971.

One interesting characteristic of the falling off in demand
for jute in the 1960's was the acquisition by manufacturers of
merchanting firms. In depressed times in the past these selling
organisations had acquired a reputation for squeezing prices down
to very low levels and partly to avoid this situation, and more
positively to try to capture additional outlets for yarn and
cloth, a number of producers engaged in forward vertical integration. In the mid 1960's, for example, H. & A. Scott acquired
Alex Laurie, Caird acquired Thomas Manning, and Wm. Halley
acquired three merchants in one year: Godfrey, Behrens, and
Swinton in 1964. In one notable case the initiative for vertical
integration came from the merchanting side. In 1960 Low Bros.,

a firm of Dundee merchants, took the initiative in creating an
enlarged group comprising one of their customers - the Forfar
firm of Don Bros. Buist. The firm subsequently expanded hori-
zontally in the jute trade by acquiring the Brechin firm of
J. & J. Smart. A further recent (1978) step in backward vertical integration has been the group's acquisition of Thiokol,
the major local supplier of extruded polypropylene tape for
weaving.

Vertical integration

This latter pattern of acquisitions has helped to produce a
situation where an increasing proportion of the jute trade is
in the hands of vertically-integrated businesses. The proportion so covered in 1946 was put at around 77% in spinning and
65% in weaving by the 1948 Board of Trade Report (para. 23).
The Restrictive Practices Court was informed in 1962 that 73%
of Dundee jute production was accounted for by firms which had
spinning, weaving and merchanting departments (L.R.4.R.P.,
p.423); and the fact that most of the company deaths of the
late 1960's and early 1970's were amongst non-integrated weaving firms contributed further to this trend.

The data in Table 2.6 below show for the period 1954-1977 the
number of firms falling into various categories of vertical
integration.

TABLE 2.6   Vertical Integration in U.K. Jute Industry
1954-1977 (No. of firms)

	Spinner-Weavers	Spinners	Weavers	Total	Spinner-Weavers/Total
1954	16	12	22	50	32%
1955	16	11	14	41	39%
1956	18	1o	14	42	43%
1957	17	9	14	40	43%
1958	15	7	13	35	43%
1959	15	7	13	35	43%
1960	15	6	11	32	47%
1961	15	5	11	31	48%
1962	15	5	1o	30	50%
1963	15	5	9	29	52%
1964	14	6	9	29	48%
1965	13	5	9	27	48%
1966	13	5	8	26	50%
1967	13	5	8	26	50%
1968	13	5	8	26	50%
1969	13	5	6	24	54%
1970	12	5	5	22	55%
1971	11	4	3	18	61%
1972	11	4	3	18	61%
1973	12	4	3	19	63%
1974	9	5	3	17	53%
1975	9	4	2	15	60%
1976	8	3	3	14	57%
1977	8	3	3	14	57%

Source :   Association of European Jute Industries Statistical
Yearbook. A.E.J.I., Paris. It may be noted that
for no obvious reason the data in the Total column
of Table 2.6 do not exactly correspond with those
in Table 2.4 above.

The other piece of information revealed by Table 2.6 is the
different death rates of various categories of firms in the
Table. Analysis of this (although it does not fully take
account of migration from one category to another in the
Table) reveals the following.

TABLE 2.7   Analysis of Death Rates of Firm Categories in
Table 2.6

	Spinner-Weavers	Spinners	Weavers	Total
1954-1977	50%	75%	86%	72%
1967-1977	38%	40%	63%	46%

Source: Table 2.6

The data in Table 2.7 confirm the considerably higher death
rates among non-integrated firms (especially weavers) compared
with integrated businesses, particularly over the period 1967-
1977.

The fate of smaller businesses

As mentioned earlier there has been a number of cases of individual businesses going into liquidation. This happened towards the end of the 1960's, and affected in particular
smaller, non-integrated weaving concerns.

In order to examine this question of "deaths" etc. in the
industry over the period of the late 1960's and early 1970's
in a little more detail a search was undertaken at Companies
House in Edinburgh in respect of those businesses which went
out of independent existence over this period. There were 12
such firms. As was noted previously a number of small firms
was acquired by large businesses. These included D. & R. Duke
of Brechin acquired by Sidlaw in 1959 and added to by John
Lowson Jr. of Forfar in 1962, and Ogilvie Bros. of Kirriemuir
acquired by J. & D. Wilkie in 1971. Both of these firms were
quite small. In 1968 Duke & Lowson employed only 300 people,
while in the same year Ogilvie Bros. employed 192.

Voluntary liquidation was, however, the most common form of
corporate death. Most of those involved were small family
businesses. W.G. Grant, for example, despite some attempt at
diversification into the building products industry went into
voluntary liquidation in 1972, having employed 380 people in
1970. Douglas Fraser & Sons of Arbroath, which in 1967 had a
capital employed of over £1m. followed the same path at an
earlier date in January 1968. These businesses were among the
larger concerns to be eliminated during this period. Others
were very much smaller non-integrated concerns specialising in
weaving. T.L. Miller, for example, with capital employed in
1968 of only £47,458, ceased jute manufacturing in 1971. The
firm continued in business with its merchanting activities,
although making considerable losses, only until 1976 when it
went into voluntary liquidation. A very similar situation
applied in the case of R.G. Kennedy & Co. (Textiles). The
company had a capital employed of £60,000 in 1968; and while
it had experienced losses for a number of years from the mid
to late 1960's it did not go into liquidation until 1971.
Don & Duncan, another non-integrated weaving concern, was larger with a capital employed of £157,773 in 1968. This firm,
which had previously manufactured jute sacking, bagging and

tarpaulins, went into liquidation in 1970.

These few details would again seem to confirm the exposed position of the small weaving concerns during this period of
change in the traditional industry.

In summary, the most obvious change in market structure has
been that the number of firms originally in the local jute
industry declined as the market as a whole contracted. This
decline was especially rapid during the period 1967-1977; it
affected particularly firms in the middle size category (employing 51-500 persons); and by far the largest "organisation-
al" category of firms to disappear were the non-integrated
businesses, particularly weavers. Mergers or acquisitions
were a characteristic of the industry. In one notable case
this involved a coming together of two firms previously in the
middle-size category. In other cases smaller businesses were
acquired by much larger concerns. Deaths in the industry
occurred because of a failure to adapt to the new industrial
textiles conditions, or an absence of family successors in the
business.

The decline of traditional jute manufacturing thus produced a
smaller, more compact and possibly concentrated industry as a
number of smaller, non-integrated constituents of the market
disappeared. The decline in the number of plants per firm
also reinforces this impression of compactness. The ratio of
establishments to enterprises in the industry, which in the
1958, 1963 and 1968 Census of Production reports stood at 1.41,
1.73 and 1.72 respectively, fell to an average of 1.18 during
the period 1970-1977, suggesting that even allowing for the incidence of smaller firms being taken over by larger ones, the
industry was rationalising itself so far as eliminating multi-
plant operations was concerned.

FURTHER CHANGES IN MARKET ENVIRONMENT

In addition to data on the formal structure of the industry
and changes therein, it is important to be aware of changes in
the structural environment of the market which were also taking
place throughout the 1960's. There were two such elements in
the industry over this period. First, the degree of import
protection administered by Jute Control together with the issue
of import protection in general. Second, the operation of the
industry's restrictive trading agreements.

Jute Control

Jute Control functioned to protect the Dundee industry in
three ways. First, there was a complete ban on the import of
non-standard goods except for carpet yarns - "excluded goods".
This lasted until 1964; and in respect of 1962 it was estimated that the ban afforded absolute protection to 80% of total
U.K. jute goods production (L.R.4R.P., p.452). Second, there
was a system of full import price equation which raised the
price of imported Indian jute goods to an ex-works level
thought to be equal to that of an efficient Dundee manufacturer.
Third, a system of partial protection was applied after 1957
to a range of goods thereafter known as the Depressed Range.
Following representations by the Indian government and producers, certain imported jute goods formerly sold by Control at
fully equated prices were sold at a fixed markup. This markup
was originally set at 30% in 1957 - compared with the former
equated price level equivalent markup of 47%. The Depressed
Range largely comprised standard Hessians for bag making; and
the markup originally set at 30% was reduced in 1960 to 20%,
and again in 1963 to 10%. The Dundee industry was also, of
course, protected by means of a normal range of tariffs from
non-Commonwealth jute imports, although these were of little
significance.

So far as the degree of import protection was concerned,
there was throughout the period of the 1950's and 1960's a
general reduction in the shelter which Control offered the
industry from Indian competition. As outlined in Chapter 1
the war-time system of Control was continued with only minor
modifications until 1954, when trading in raw jute was returned
to private hands. Imported jute goods, however, remained
under Control, and these were sold at equated or markup prices,
which were held to represent prices with which an efficient
Dundee manufacturer could compete. The actual markup depended
upon the class of goods; and while for some categories held
to be of importance to the continuance of the Dundee industry
the markup was maintained at 45% until the termination of the
whole system in May 1969, there were some ranges where the
markup had been reduced to 20% in 1960, and some categories
(e.g. heavy sacks) where the only protection was a very limited
quota system.

In August 1963 a major change was instituted by which previously excluded goods, that is goods in respect of which the
Dundee industry had hitherto enjoyed complete protection, were
to be imported by Control and marked up by 50%. At the same
time the markup on common Hessians was further reduced from
20% to 10% (Board of Trade Journal, 16.8.63, pp.328-9). A
year later, in September 1964, the markup on these Hessians
was eliminated, and arrangements were made for trade in them

to be returned to private hands; while, in respect of those
goods previously marked up at 50%, the markup was reduced to
45% in some cases, and to around 35% in others (Board of Trade
Journal, 4.9.64, pp.502-3). From May 1969 Jute Control's
function of marking up the prices of imported jute goods was
terminated; and was replaced by a quota system which placed
purely physical limits on the import of such goods (Board of
Trade Journal, 6.12.69, pp.1519-21).

Following the entry of the U.K. into the E.E.C. in 1973 new
Jute Arrangements were concluded which preserved the position
of India and Bangladesh vis-à-vis Britain. The common external tariff applied by existing E.E.C. members to such imports
continued to apply, but at a reduced rate. Absolute import
quotas, however, also apply to the remainder of the E.E.C.
countries, and are the sole source of protection for U.K. manufacturers. Currently the level of these is part of the discussions within the context of the Multi Fibre Arrangement
between the E.E.C. and the developing countries of the Far
East.

Opinions have varied as to the impact of this protection or
its removal on the Dundee industry. On the one hand it could
be argued that other changes were taking place which had the
effect of ousting jute from traditional market areas and which
import restrictions could do little to mitigate. Such, for
example, may have been the case with the increased use of
paper or polythene bags. There was also little which any form
of import protection could do to reduce the trend to bulk
transporting or containerisation of the 1960's. On the other
hand the trade felt it was necessary to maintain a degree of
protection for Dundee manufacturers. What tended to happen,
the industry feared, was that as protection was "lowered" in
one range of goods so manufacturers of technically adjacent
goods suffered. The final impact, it might thus be argued,
of one reduction in markup would be felt across other grades
of cloth where markup had not been altered.

Appendix Tables 2.3 and 2.4 indicate the level of import penetration for jute yarn and cloth respectively for the period
1951-1977. From these one might have expected to be able to
detect some influence of the various changes in the degree of
import protection offered by Jute Control. Looking at the 3-year
moving average data in particular, for yarn these indicate an
unusual pattern of a fall in import penetration up to the late
1950's, a rise from this time until a peak of 3.4% in the mid
1960's, after which the figures fall off to a slightly lower
plateau of 1.5%-2.5% for the remainder of the period. With
regard to jute goods, a more obvious pattern emerges, although

not one which might have been expected in the light of Control
regulations. In the case of cloth, import penetration fell
from its 1951 level until a low point in the mid 1960's, from
which it rose significantly - a rise which could be explained
by the 1963 and 1964 reductions in import protection. A
further trend which appears significant is the rise in the
level of cloth import penetration as the whole U.K. jute
industry declined (see Appendix Table 2.6). This does not
appear to have arisen from any change in the level of exports,
which, excluding 1976, averaged around 14% of production for
the 1970's, but from a rapid rise in the volume of imports
themselves. It may be that this is further evidence of a
point taken up again later in this chapter, that as the traditional jute industry seemed bound to decline significantly
sooner or later as polypropylene increasingly ousted jute
from successive previous end-use markets, U.K. jute manufacturers, who had significant interests in polypropylene, did not
necessarily seek to fight any rearguard action on the part of
jute in the dimension of price competition, but rather enjoyed
what were acknowledged inevitably to be jute's last years.
This absence of more aggressive competition in jute by Dundee
producers as the jute industry declined may be an important
explanation for the historically high and increasing levels
of import penetration in the 1970's in respect of cloth.

Quite in addition to the more concrete arguments regarding
import protection, a further not insignificant effect of Jute
Control was that the whole system contributed to a cohesive-
ness within the industry, which must have broken down as
Control's function was gradually eliminated. Thus (Jackson,
1979, p.111):

> "One further, very important consequence of
> protection must be mentioned. The system of
> equated prices, involving as it did the cal-
> culation and publication of a price at which
> imported goods were to be sold, facilitated
> the construction of price agreements among
> home producers, so that for an important part
> of production there was an absence of price
> competition, not only between Indian and
> Dundee goods, but also between the goods of
> one Dundee producer and another."

It is, of course, in this last sense that Control performed a
function similar to that of the industry's trade pricing
agreements. Insofar as this is true, then it may also have
contributed to what a former member of the industry referred
to as a "management desensitisation" over the years from 1945

to the early 1960's. This was, by implication, a period over
which management was protected from the full impact of foreign
competition, when domestic rivalry was similarly muted, and
when many small firm managements were relieved of having to
make any real decisions upon pricing at all.

Trade pricing agreements

As mentioned above, the other major change in the industry's
structural environment was the ending of the network of domestic trade pricing agreements in March 1963 following a
Restrictive Practices Court decision. These agreements had
grown up along with the system of Control; and the argument
for their retention was largely based upon the inability of
Control fully to carry out its functions without the existence
of the industry's own network of delivered common price agreements. Control had produced a situation during the war in
which it was necessary to have common prices of jute goods in
respect of imports and Dundee-produced goods, so that any jute
goods user possessing the appropriate Certificate of Approval
to obtain jute cloth or yarn should pay the same price regardless of whether Control allocated to him imported or home-
produced goods. This means of ensuring an equitable allocation
of scarce wartime goods was extended after 1945 to become a
system for protecting the Dundee industry from import competition. Such imports were sold through Control at a price which
was "equated" or brought into line with that of a notionally
efficient Dundee manufacturer; and the mechanism was later
simplified by adopting a standard markup for various categories
of imported jute goods. In order to arrive at "fair" equated
prices both Control and the jute trade association employed
independent firms of accountants to determine prices and to
monitor manufacturer profitability.

In the industry's view, it was necessary to have, as an adjunct to the formal system of Control, a set of price agreements among domestic producers. These agreements, in the
words of the Low & Bonar chairman (Low & Bonar, 1960 Annual
Report), were "the necessary lubricating oil which makes the
unusual and somewhat involved form of protection (i.e. Control)
work smoothly and efficiently". The chairman of Jute Industries further reflected the general view in the trade in
stating (Financial Times, 23.1.61), "We feel strongly that
these agreements play an indispensable part in the general
structure of protection for the U.K. industry as an essential
support for the operations of the Jute Control". It thus
appears to have been the industry's clear view that the intention of Control, safeguarded by strict monitoring of producer
costs and profits, was to eliminate import and domestic

competition. All that the seven registered trading agreements
among domestic producers did was to translate Control's super-
vision of jute manufacturers' ex-works prices into a common
price system covering delivered prices and merchanting activities such as folding and baling of cloth. Without these additional arrangements "improper" price competition would have
occurred among manufacturers. Thus in the words of the industry's most significant witness at the Restrictive Practices
Court hearing (Robertson, 1962, p.98) :

> "We say that this is the case because were there
> no such complex of agreements to ensure uniform
> delivered prices to consumers, then the system
> of import and release of jute goods from India
> and from Pakistan which the Jute Control oper-
> ates would be incomplete as a protective
> measure, would be frustrated in its intentions
> or would have to be discontinued by reason of
> difficulties which would arise; for, in the
> absence of agreements, partly owing to market
> fluctuations and partly because of the detailed
> method of pricing used by the Jute Control, im-
> ported goods would be available to consumers
> (against the Jute Control's intentions) at
> prices lower than those which the Board of
> Trade acknowledges as appropriate to efficient
> United Kingdom producers."

In terms of the Act under which the case was decided upon,
the industry also argued that in the absence of the pricing
agreements there would be a considerable reduction in the
size of the industry; and given the significance of the jute
industry in Dundee - it accounted for 35% of manufacturing
employees in the city - there would be a considerable increase in unemployment in what was regarded as being a one-
industry town. In addition to these major points the industry
also argued that in the absence of the trading agreements jute
goods users would face a reduction in the range of specialist
goods available and an increase in their price, that the flex-
ibility to users of having an industry on one's doorstep would
be lost, that the level of users' stockholding would have to
rise, and that the system of common price agreements not only
saved customers' time in not having to "shop around" to find
the lowest price, but was also responsible for creating an
environment which had encouraged manufacturers to invest considerable sums of money in new capital equipment which had an
impact in keeping down price levels.

These arguments were, however, opposed by the Counsel for the

Registrar of Restrictive Trading Agreements. He argued that
the presence of the registered agreements prevented the most
efficient firms or specialist merchants from expanding through
price competition, and that fixed-price trading agreements
sheltered high-cost producers, maintained excess capacity in
the industry, and reduced the incentive to firms in general to
seek out low-cost methods of manufacture. On 26th March 1963
the Court under Lord Cameron gave its judgement. It did not
believe that the delivered-price agreements were a necessary
adjunct to Jute Control to prevent an undue contraction of the
industry. It did not accept that administratively Control
would find it impossible to arrive at correct equated or markup prices without the trade association agreements. Nor was
the Court convinced that the abandonment of the agreements
would necessarily bring about a significant increase in unemployment in the area. As a result of this finding by the Court
the agreements ceased to operate from that date.

What should not be lost sight of in the midst of the detailed
material above is the potential impact of these changes on the
industry. The relaxation of import controls and the abolition
of the trading agreements obviously increased the degree of
international and domestic competition faced by Dundee producers. One would, therefore, expect pressure upon smaller
marginal firms - often non-integrated concerns - to increase.
These businesses could either cease production altogether or
accept an offer of acquisition by a larger company. Either
alternative would lead not only to a slimming down of the
industry but also to increased market concentration. Such
increased concentration might also follow from the freedom for
competitive pricing among domestic producers in the absence of
trade pricing agreements. Given the larger financial resources,
and possibly also the greater efficiency of the larger as
opposed to the smallest firms, the former would benefit from
any increased price competition in terms of improved market
share. Finally, the uncertainty of the new competitive environment of the early 1960's might have been expected to lead to
more forward integration in the market, to a reduced commitment
to long-term capital projects in the jute industry, and for
some businesses, to a positive plan to diversify into market
areas offering more profits, growth or security.

Assessment

Very little work has been done by way of assessing the outcome
specifically of the ending of protection or the trading agreements in the industry. The view of McDowall, Draper and
McGuinness (1976, p.50) was that "It is probably no exaggerat-
ion to say that only the Jute Control with its import bans and

markups stood between the British jute industry and virtual
extinction in the 1950's and early 1960's". With regard to
the outcome of the ending of the trading agreements, spokesmen
of the trade feared (Low & Bonar, 1961 Annual Report) that
"their rejection by the Court would create a difficult situation"; while the feeling in the industry after the Court's
decision was that a considerable strain had thereby been placed
upon individual firms by each having subsequently to make
economic decisions within its own commercial environment
(Dundee Chamber, Dec. 1964, p.241). With regard to import
protection, although the total withdrawal of the system by
1960 may well have had a considerable impact upon the Dundee
industry, the fact is that the system was very gradually dis-
mantled over more than a decade from 1954 to 1969. This was a
decade, too, during which there were other significant changes
taking place within the industry. This was particularly the
case in respect of technical substitution in former jute end-
use markets; and this situation led the industry's N.E.D.C.
to conclude (N.E.D.C., 1970) that "any increase in (jute) imports following quota revisions is likely (in its impact) to
be small compared to the inroads into the domestic market
made by polypropylene". In respect of the ending of the manufacturers' common pricing agreements in 1963, more research
has been carried out. The results, however, are inconclusive
as regards attributing any subsequent events specifically to
this cause. Hamilton, in his thesis on this aspect of the
industry, points to the geographical concentration of the
market, the continuation of the function of Control after 1963,
the healthy state of demand from carpet manufacturers up to
1967, the general absence of excess capacity among producers,
the operation of an informal price information agreement within the industry, and the role of the largest firms as price
leaders. All of these conditions, the author concludes,
served to dilute the pro-competitive impact of the Restrictive
Practices Court's decision; and his "principal conclusion"
(Hamilton, 1974) was that the Court decision "had little or no
impact upon the jute industry". These two events must,
however, be seen as contributing to the generally changed environment of the jute industry over the 1960's; and although
it is recognised that it would be difficult to ascribe particular consequences to either of them alone, this does not mean
to say that their impact upon the industry can be ignored.

CONCLUSIONS

This chapter has dealt with the two principal changes in
structure in the traditional Dundee jute industry over the
past 20 or 30 years. These were analysed under the headings
of changing markets, and changes in market structure -

narrowly and broadly defined.

The context of this whole study is one of the decline of a
traditional fibre market as the data in Table 2.1 indicate.
One can see the causes of this in three distinct areas.
Declining use of products with which jute was associated, and
upon which it was at one time heavily dependent (linoleum);
displacement of jute from use in a market where the jute-user
product has continued to be successful (tufted carpets, where
woven polypropylene has taken over as the primary backing
material and where polypropylene is also displacing jute in
woven carpets); and elimination of jute itself as a means of
directly fulfilling certain functions (the case of jute bags
and wrappings being displaced by bulk handling and containerisation). These changes came about at different times, at
different speeds, and for different reasons. The response of
the jute industry has necessarily been different in each case.

The "derived" demand for jute in the linoleum market was the
first to go. It began to disappear from the late 1950's onwards; and the speed of decline may be gauged from the fact
that U.K. linoleum output declined from its post-war peak of
51.6m.sq.m. in 1955 to 20.8m.sq.m. in 1965 - a decline of 60%
over this period. This market was lost to jute fairly rapidly
on the basis of changed consumer tastes away from hard floorcoverings, and as, with the advent of tufting, carpets came
within the household budget of an increasing part of the population. Under these circumstances, the members of the jute
industry lost a market which was beyond their control. The
one fortunate aspect of this particular transition was that,
at least initially, the new growth area of tufted carpets
supplied the jute industry with a significant replacement for
its lost linoleum market.

More dramatic in scale and speed was the elimination of jute
from the highly attractive market for the primary backing of
tufted carpets. This was a phenomenon of the later 1960's;
and from still possessing 71% of this market in 1968 (representing an output of 35.1m.sq.m.), jute's share fell to 12% in
1972 (9.2m.sq.m.) (Grilli, 1974, pp.17-18). Here the displacement of jute occurred for a mixture of technological and price
reasons. With respect to basic developments in man-made fibre
technology, the jute manufacturers cannot, of course, be held
responsible for these. There does seem to be a general feeling,
however, that high prices for jute goods (including the role of
Jute Control in the U.K.) did stimulate the fibre applications
of polypropylene. Thus according to a United Nations F.A.O.
study (1969),

"Fears about the long-term future availability
of jute and jute goods, and the present incon-
veniences of short-term fluctuations in supplies
and prices, have led jute users to welcome the
development of domestic substitutes which are
free from these drawbacks. And the high price
of jute goods in developed countries has made
the development of such a substitute economic-
ally feasible. In addition to these general
factors, there are several specific factors in
the bag and the carpet backing markets which
have encouraged synthetic substitutes for jute,
but these are of less importance than the
general considerations outlined above."

On the question of price disparity, the World Bank study concluded (Grilli, 1974, p.14) that "In general, price different-
ials between jute and polypropylene replacement fabrics
widened substantially in the late sixties and early seventies,
to the point where direct price competition between jute and
synthetics became almost impossible".

In this instance of displacement the manufacturers in the
traditional Dundee market, realising the trend of events which
set in during the late 1960's, have largely moved into the
displacing technology. The speed with which this move was
accomplished, and the degree of involvement in polymer technology, have each varied from firm to firm. Some of the original jute businesses realised fairly rapidly that polypropylene was to be the fibre which would replace jute in many
areas, and that it was the one to which they should turn for
commercial survival. A number of these firms thus not only
use polypropylene tape, but actually extrude polypropylene
film for "chips" or granules themselves - slitting the film
to produce tape. Thus Low & Bonar and Sidlaw established
polytape in 1966; and other local firms such as H. & A.
Scott also established extruding facilities. At the other
extreme there were businesses which hung back from entering
the new market on such a large scale, and which only entered
the weaving sector, using tape produced by specialist extrusion facilities established locally by Thiokol (formerly a
subsidiary of W.G. Grace of America, but now owned by the
local firm of Don Bros. Buist) and Filtrona (owned over the
period of this study by Bunzl Pulp & Paper Co.). In all,
however, Dundee appears to have exerted such a locational
force in the provision of polypropylene for weaving into a
variety of uses that an estimated two-thirds of such United
Kingdom polypropylene production is now carried out in the

Dundee area, including Forfar (Dundee Courier and Advertiser,
9.2.77).

It has been pointed out in the context of other research
(McDowall and Draper, 1978, p.34) that the involvement of the
traditional Dundee jute industry in polypropylene may even
have contributed to the rapid succession of the latter to the
markets of the former. That is, Dundee jute producers, being
involved in the expanding polypropylene market, did not have
the incentive which specialist jute producers would have had
to fight a determined rearguard action on the part of jute by
means of keen pricing. Rather they were willing to enjoy what
were inevitably the last years of profits of jute in the
knowledge that they had safely entered the market for polypropylene which was replacing the traditional fibre. Thus
McDowall and Draper point out that in the late 1960's and
early 1970's polypropylene replaced jute more rapidly in
Europe than in the United States, although as polypropylene
cloth prices were slightly higher in Europe than America one
might have expected the opposite to be the case. Thus despite
polypropylene cloth being more expensive in Europe than in the
U.S., its price advantage against jute (the proportion by
which the price of polypropylene was less than that of jute)
was 45% in the U.K. in respect of primary carpet backing cloth
compared with 23% in the U.S. in 1972. British jute producers
thus seem not to have made any efforts themselves by way of
price competition to stem the tide of polypropylene; and the
result was that for primary tufted carpet backing jute's share
of the market in 1976 in the U.K. was 3% while in the U.S. it
was 20%.

The market for jute bags, wrappings and other minor end uses
(such as the household furnishing trade) fell away rather less
dramatically to new technologies and substitute products. The
trend towards bulk handling and containerisation - essentially
the result of new materials-handling engineering, and a response to higher wage costs involved in traditional systems -
affected different commodities and different economies at
varying times. In this area too, however, a major change
occurred over the period from the late 1960's to the early
1970's; and again polypropylene was a significant cause of
jute's reduced markets. For example, over the period 1968-
1971 jute's share of the free world bag and sack market fell
from 88% of the total to 67%. Even this apparently modest
proportional reduction in market share resulted in a virtual
halving of jute output to this area - from 31,000 tonnes per
annum to 16,000 tonnes (Grilli, 1974, pp.17-18). The response
by the jute manufacturers in this market area has correspondingly been to enter the market for polypropylene bags - a

strategy which Scott & Robertson among the local producers
have particularly followed.

Regarding changes in market structure, the data here are
fairly informative. We can trace the slimming down of the
size of the traditional industry by total numbers and with
reference to the size distribution of firms; and on the basis
of local knowledge we can distinguish among disappearances
between "deaths" and "acquisitions", and also identify the
acquiring firms in respect of the latter category. As one
might expect, the number of firms in the industry fell considerably over the years 1945-1977 - particularly over the
last decade of the period. The firms which have disappeared
altogether (as opposed to simply leaving the jute industry)
to engage totally or largely in synthetics) have predominantly been small and/or non-integrated concerns. At the level of
casual observation (in contrast to the basis of statistical
testing employed in Chapter 4), size would appear to be an
important determinant of survival.

Of concern to the industrial economist, one might want to
know what happened to competition among firms over the period
studied. Undoubtedly this was muted by the existence of Jute
Control and the industry's domestic trade pricing agreements.
It was noted, too, that the effects of these continued until
the mid to late 1960's. One would suggest therefore that,
ceteris paribus, growth of the more efficient firms at the
expense of the less so was restricted, and marginal firms
survived in the industry which would otherwise have been
eliminated. It was also undoubtedly the function of these
arrangements to allow the industry to sustain a higher level
of profitability than would otherwise have been the case.
The demise of these arrangements coincided with the occurrence
of technological market competition from polypropylene. That
the synthetic fibre was so rapidly adopted by a large proportion of the trade is one indication of its competitive potential vis-à-vis jute. At the same time this mixture of natural
and synthetic output by most firms in the industry prevents
one from using aggregated profitability data (rates of return
on capital employed, or sales margins) to measure the extent
of competition. One can imagine that with the continuance in
business of a number of older firms, the downturn in total
demand for yarn and jute goods from the late 1960's onwards
created a buyers market. As in most markets, however, the extent to which firms experienced increased competition varied
from one sector of the jute market to another. While demand
for woven carpets remained strong, the spinning of high quality carpet yarns continued to be profitable, and those firms
which specialised in this technologically more demanding

sector and which enjoyed something of a technological barrier
to entry (Sidlaw, Scott & Robertson, Thomson Shepherd, and
the C.W.S. Taybank Jute Works) enjoyed success beyond the end
of the 1960's. This situation may be contrasted with the view
of the chairman of Craiks, a small Forfar business now owned
by Low & Bonar, who complained by the late 1960's (Craiks,
1967 Annual Report) "Not only have we had to contend with a
steady falling off in demand, but with a serious and widespread wave of price cutting, resulting in the whittling away
of already slender profit margins". This sort of comment,
together with the exit from the market of an increasing
number of smaller, marginal firms at the turn of the decade,
suggests that competitive pressures were increasing - although
it should again be emphasised that the source of these was
technological change which originated outwith the traditional
jute industry. It is with the way in which the firms in
general dealt with this outside source of pressure to which
we now turn in the following chapter under the heading of
diversification.

Appendix Table 2.1

U.K. Jute Industry Output ('000 tonnes)

	Yarn	Cloth	Raw Jute Consumption*
1945	75.1	49.2	73.1
1946	90.4	52.8	89.1
1947	96.8	57.7	96.4
1948	101.9	59.9	101.6
1949	90.1	51.6	89.9
1950	107.1	64.5	108.9
1951	116.4	69.0	113.7
1952	108.0	65.0	106.7
1953	133.8	77.8	132.2
1954	139.8	82.2	137.7
1955	146.8	87.5	145.6
1956	144.5	90.1	142.1
1957	140.0	82.0	139.6
1958	127.2	73.1	124.0
1959	139.8	81.2	137.2
1960	144.1	83.5	141.4
1961	117.4	69.9	116.7
1962	131.9	78.2	130.7
1963	135.9	81.4	134.7
1964	132.9	78.8	131.1
1965	129.5	75.7	128.9
1966	122.8	73.1	122.4
1967	113.8	64.6	113.8
1968	111.5	59.7	110.8
1969	107.9	52.7	107.7
1970	87.5	40.9	86.7
1971	77.6	32.0	77.7
1972	74.7	26.5	77.2
1973	68.2	24.2	68.9
1974	57.5	20.9	59.3
1975	51.1	16.3	52.5
1976	52.7	16.1	51.9
1977	46.8	13.8	46.3

* Home consumption

Note: all years are 52-week periods.

Source: Annual Abstract of Statistics. H.M.S.O., London.

Appendix Table 2.2

U.K. Manufacturers' Sales of Carpets and Rugs and Linoleum

		Carpets & Rugs*		
	Woven Wool	Tufted	Other	Linoleum*
1945	4.0	0.3		15.3
1946	13.0	1.3		22.9
1947	19.2	1.9		25.1
1948	24.8	2.5		35.9
1949	28.4	2.8		43.1
1950	32.9	3.4		42.8
1951	31.5	4.3		38.8
1952	31.4	4.1		31.1
1953	34.7	6.6		38.6
1954	38.5	7.5		49.2
1955	37.7	6.9		51.6
1956	33.9	7.6		46.4
1957	37.1	3.3	8.1	46.5
1958	38.2	4.9	8.4	47.2
1959	38.1	7.5	7.8	48.7
1960	38.5	9.8	9.0	47.8
1961	35.7	11.1	9.0	42.4
1962	34.9	12.8	12.0	38.0
1963	34.9	..	13.7	30.9
1964	36.1	27.8	16.1	29.2
1965	33.7	32.2	18.6	20.8
1966	32.8	36.0	17.6	16.7
1967	29.8	44.1	18.2	13.5
1968	33.4	49.7	20.0	11.2
1969	32.8	52.9	25.3	8.9
1970	31.8	60.7	26.8	7.2
1971	31.4	70.7	29.7	6.1
1972	33.4	89.7	27.7	5.2
1973	32.6	102.2	27.8	5.6
1974	27.1	102.8	27.3	4.6
1975	25.4	109.7	26.1	4.0
1976	24.1	127.8	24.9	3.9
1977	23.1	123.4	22.7	3.6

*   million sq. metres (1 sq. yd.= 0.836 sq. metres)

..   not available

Source :   Annual Abstract of Statistics.   H.M.S.O., London.

Appendix Table 2.3

U.K. Jute Yarn Imports and Exports ('000 tonnes)

	Imports	Production	Exports	Imports/ Home Consumption (%)	
1951	4.9	116.4	3.2	4.1	
1952	0.3	108.0	2.1	0.3	2.6*
1953	4.7	133.8	2.1	3.4	2.6
1954	5.9	139.8	2.2	4.1	3.1
1955	2.8	146.8	3.0	1.9	2.1
1956	0.5	144.5	2.8	0.4	1.2
1957	1.7	140.0	3.9	1.2	1.0
1958	1.6	127.2	2.9	1.3	1.5
1959	2.8	139.8	2.7	2.0	1.8
1960	3.0	144.1	2.7	2.1	2.2
1961	2.8	117.4	3.4	2.4	2.5
1962	3.8	131.9	4.1	2.9	2.6
1963	3.2	135.9	4.1	2.4	2.7
1964	3.8	132.9	3.3	2.8	3.1
1965	5.3	129.5	3.0	4.0	3.4
1966	4.2	122.8	2.4	3.4	2.9
1967	1.5	113.8	1.8	1.3	1.9
1968	1.2	111.5	1.5	1.1	1.5
1969	2.2	107.9	1.8	2.0	1.5
1970	1.3	87.5	1.8	1.5	1.8
1971	1.5	77.6	1.4	1.9	2.4
1972	2.8	74.7	2.7	3.7	2.6
1973	1.5	68.2	3.0	2.2	2.4
1974	0.8	57.5	3.0	1.4	1.3
1975	0.2	51.1	2.4	0.4	1.5
1976	1.3	51.7	3.7	2.6	2.7
1977	2.3	46.8	3.0	5.0	

* 3-year moving average

Source: Association of European Jute Industries Statistical Yearbook. A.E.J.I., Paris.

Appendix Table 2.4

U.K. Jute Cloth Imports and Exports ('000 tonnes)

	Imports	Production	Exports	Imports/ Home Consumption (%)	
1951	94.9	69.0	12.8	62.8	
1952	56.8	65.0	11.8	51.6	53.7*
1953	59.5	77.8	9.9	46.7	51.1
1954	87.7	82.2	10.3	54.9	50.1
1955	71.2	87.5	12.5	48.7	49.4
1956	60.9	90.1	14.2	44.5	44.7
1957	49.7	82.0	10.9	41.0	43.8
1958	54.3	73.1	9.2	45.9	44.9
1959	64.5	81.2	10.5	47.7	47.1
1960	65.8	83.5	11.5	47.8	46.5
1961	47.1	69.9	10.1	44.1	45.2
1962	51.9	78.2	11.4	43.7	43.1
1963	49.0	81.4	12.1	41.4	41.8
1964	50.8	78.8	11.0	40.4	37.6
1965	43.3	75.7	8.7	30.9	37.5
1966	46.3	73.1	7.3	41.3	40.7
1967	50.3	64.6	5.5	50.0	47.3
1968	54.9	59.7	6.2	50.6	49.8
1969	43.6	52.7	6.7	48.7	50.5
1970	39.1	40.9	5.0	52.1	51.8
1971	32.1	32.0	5.3	54.6	54.0
1972	27.7	26.5	4.1	55.3	56.3
1973	29.7	24.2	3.6	59.0	57.3
1974	25.4	20.9	2.2	57.6	58.9
1975	20.9	16.3	2.3	60.0	62.5
1976	23.1	15.8	5.9	70.0	66.3
1977	26.2	13.8	2.1	69.0	

* 3-year moving average

Source : as in Appendix Table 2.3

Appendix Table 2.5

U.K. Jute Yarn Import Penetration (%)

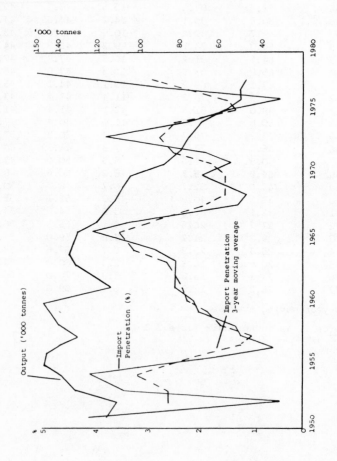

Appendix Table 2.6

U.K. Jute Cloth Import Penetration (%)

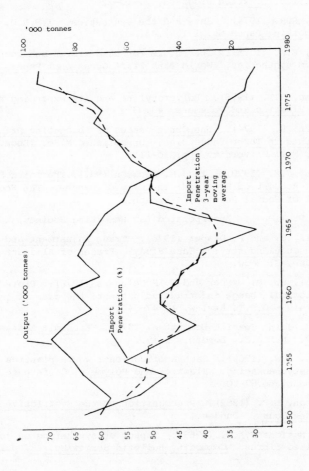

References

Board of Trade (1948). Report of Jute Working Party.
H.M.S.O., London.

Dundee Chamber of Commerce Journal. Chamber of Commerce,
Dundee.

Financial Times. Financial Times, London.

Gay, R.S. and J.A. Jenkins (1970). Industrial applications
of textiles. Textile Progress, 2, 10-22.

Grilli, E.R. (1974). Jute and the synthetics. I.B.R.D.
Staff Working Paper No. 171, p.43.

Grilli, E.R. (1975). The future for hard fibres and competition from synthetics. World Bank Staff Occasional Papers No.
19.

Grayling, J.T. (1975). Polypropylene and its expanding hori-
zons. Plastics and Polymers, 43, 37.

Hamilton, L. (1974). The Consequences of Abrogating Price
Agreements in Three Industries. Unpublished M.Sc. (Econ.)
Thesis, Hull University. pp.210-11.

Jackson, J.M. (1979). In J.M. Jackson (Ed.), The Third Statistical Account of Scotland: The City of Dundee. The Scottish
Council of Social Service, Arbroath.

L.R.4R.P. (1964). Incorporated Law Reporting Society, London.

McDowall, S. and P. Draper (1978). Trade Adjustment and the
British Jute Industry: A Case Study. Fraser of Allander
Institute, Glasgow.

McDowall, S., P. Draper and T. McGuinness (1976). Protection,
technological change and trade adjustment: the case of jute
in Britain. O.D.I. Review, 1, 47-8.

N.E.D.C. Joint Textile Committee (1970). Economic Assessment
to 1972. N.E.D.C., London. p.19.

Overton, B.W. (1969). Sack applications: woven plastics for
heavy-duty packaging. Plastics and Polymers, Conference
Supplement, pp.87-90.

Robertson, L.F. (1962). Precognition to the Restrictive
Practices Court. Dundee.

United Nations F.A.O. (1969). Impact of synthetics on jute
and allied fibres. Commodity Bulletin Series No. 46, p.11.

CHAPTER 3

DIVERSIFICATION

INTRODUCTION

As mentioned in the Introduction to this study, the term
Diversification has been adopted here to refer to the conduct
or behaviour of firms in the industry. As such the term
covers a wide spectrum of strategies and attendant issues
raised in analysing the behaviour of firms in a market, demand
for whose traditional product was under attack both from cheap
traditional imports and from new technology in the U.K. itself.

The plan of this chapter is to analyse broadly the response of
the former jute firms to the competitive forces mentioned
above, to offer short case studies of the progress of a few
individual companies, to conduct some statistical tests on
company accounting data as they relate to the performance in
diversification of the firms, and finally to attempt to draw
some conclusions.

The term diversification refers to a strategy on the part of
a business firm which takes the company into market areas not
directly related to its existing business. Thus, some of the
more obvious forms of business expansion such as manufacturing
what was previously bought in, or cases of manufacturers
moving into distribution, are referred to as vertical integration; and the term diversification is normally reserved
for corporate strategies which involve entering totally new
markets.

There appears to have been a trend towards diversification
over a large part of British industry during the past twenty
years; and "diversified" enterprises now account for a large
part of industrial output (Gorecki, 1975). What is more

interesting are the reasons for this general trend throughout
the economy, and for the policy of diversification on the part
of individual businesses. The economist must also of course
be concerned with the implications of such policies for
resource allocation in the economy as a whole.

In respect of individual firms, diversification is normally
pursued as a means of achieving a higher growth rate than may
be attained within a single market, as a means of reducing the
riskiness of earnings associated with dependence upon a single
product range, or as a means of escaping from total dependence
upon a market which is facing decline. Diversification in this
last case may obviously be a prelude to complete exit from a
market; and it is with precisely this general situation of
diversification in the face of market decline that one is con-
fronted in the case of the Dundee jute industry.

It is recognised in studies of the "jute" industry during the
1960's that a major effort was even then being made by firms
to diversify in some broad sense. Leveson (1973), for example,
refers to diversification as "perhaps the most important post
war development", and instances both the trend towards manufacturing jute products not in competition with the Calcutta
mills, and also the adoption of man-made fibres - predominantly
polypropylene - to fulfil needs traditionally met by jute.
More recently some of the textile manufacturers have been
building up their interests in engineering (some of it geared
to North Sea oil exploration and drilling), and in activities
ancillary to textiles, such as space dyeing. The result of
the former type of diversification within jute, again using
Leveson's estimates, was that the Dundee industry moved from
a situation in 1950 where it was predominantly dependent upon
packaging and sacking to one by the mid-1960's where such end
uses accounted for only about 6% of total output. This change
meant that the local industry was much more able to withstand
competition from Indian goods; and this was particularly so
in respect of the floorcoverings market, where broad cloth of
consistently high quality was required for tufted carpet
backing. More recently of course the trend has been for former jute businesses to diversify out of this area altogether.

    INDUSTRY RESPONSE

Over the period 1945-1977 the total number of firms in what
was traditionally the Dundee jute industry fell from 37 to 14.
Thus, although the predominant response to the industry's
decline has been "death" (i.e. firms ceasing to remain as
independent businesses either through total demise or as a
result of takeover), a number of firms has survived. Indeed

the number of continuing businesses is greater than suggested
above on the basis of A.J.S.M. membership, the resignation of
some continuing firms from the Association reflecting the
diminished importance of jute in their total activities rather
than the complete demise of the businesses. Thus, for example,
to the 14 full A.J.S.M. members of 1977 one should add back
three former full members which continued in business, though
without having any jute interests.

Concentrating on continuing businesses, and examining the
period from the mid 1960's onwards, it is possible to categor-
ise the response of these firms to traditional market decline
as follows.

TABLE 3.1   Response of Continuing Firms to U.K. Jute Industry
            Decline

Continuation of traditional business	Traditionalism
Partial adoption of new technology	Hesitancy
Full adoption of new technology	Innovation
Seeking of new outlets for traditional product	Reorientation
Diversification into "related" fields	Diversification
Diversification into "unrelated" fields	Conglomeration

Although these categories include most of the policies
followed by the original jute manufacturing firms, many of the
businesses involved have, often simultaneously, followed more
than one policy. The categories are therefore not mutually
exclusive, nor has it been possible to measure realistically
the proportion of the total industry at any one time falling
into any particular category. The titles in the right-hand
column of Table 3.1 are adopted for "shorthand" purposes in
the following paragraphs. The problem with trying to measure
in any exact way this type of behaviour is not simply one of
devising watertight compartments into which firms can be placed,
but also that of putting accurate dates upon events and
measuring the significance within a firm's total business of
certain ventures without the aid of data breaking down company
sales or turnover.

Within these limitations, however, and in terms of the 17
firms which continued in independent existence from the early
1960's to 1977, one can suggest the following breakdown into
the categories outlined in Table 3.1.

TABLE 3.2   Responses of Individual Firms

Category	Number	%
Traditionalism	4	24
Hesitancy	1	6
Innovation	7	41
Reorientation	1.5*	9
Diversification	2	12
Conglomeration	1.5*	9
	17	101**

*   the response of Sidlaw has been equally divided between these two categories

**   due to rounding

Perhaps surprising is the proportion of firms (around a quarter) which have continued in the traditional business of jute spinning and weaving - either spinning woven carpet yarns or weaving cloth for a variety of uses. The explanation, however, is that one of these firms is a subsidiary of a larger enterprise which provides the Traditionalist with a captive market (the Victoria Spinning Co. is a subsidiary of woven carpet makers B.M.K.). Of the other three firms in this category, one is in a state of decline resulting from a reduction in orders from established sources, competition in the traditional fibre from more aggressive firms which although having wider interests still produce woven carpet yarn and cloth, and displacement by polypropylene. In fact this firm (Buist Spinning Co.) closed down in 1979 and its premises were acquired by Scott & Robertson. The second of these three firms, Wm. Cleghorn, employs some 30 people very largely in preparing jute waste for use as roofing felt. The third enterprise is the Taybank Jute Works of the C.W.S. In common with the remainder of the industry in general, the scale of operations at Taybank has contracted over recent years. Employment, however, fell by only around 25% in the decade to 1977; and in that year the firm employed 415 persons in spinning and weaving. Although the firm was at one time heavily vertically integrated with the Co-operative movement (with a large output of coal and flour bags), 98% of turnover is now accounted for by non-Co-operative sales. Of spinning capacity, two-thirds is for woven carpet wefts, in which market Taybank is estimated to be the third largest producer after Sidlaw and Scott & Robertson. The remaining one-third of spinning output goes to weaving: half to the firm's own looms, half to weavers with none or insufficient spinning capacity. Taybank's own woven output goes overwhelmingly (around 75%) to the roofing felt trade, with smaller

amounts going to car-assembly, brattice cloth and minor packaging end uses. This unit has thus survived without adopting
polypropylene technology by modernising its spinning capacity
to serve the woven carpet industry, and concentrating woven
jute output in non-standard markets for which the scale of
demand does not attract Indian competition, and in respect of
which polypropylene is not presently a substitute. This strategy could not, of course, have been followed by all firms.
Traditionalism has, nonetheless, allowed one or two units,
including a relatively large employer such as Taybank, to survive in a rapidly contracting market.

The category of Hesitancy includes only one firm; but is of
more than passing interest. The situation is one where the
firm concerned has undertaken weaving of polypropylene bags
on jute-weaving machinery. This has obviously minimised the
commitment (financial and technological) of the firm to the
new fibre; and although it is possible only to produce relatively unsophisticated goods using this approach (mail bags
and coal sacks etc.) this partial adoption of the new technology has allowed one firm to survive.

The vast bulk of the former jute spinning and weaving firms
which have survived have done so by fully adopting the new
technology of polypropylene. These innovators in our termin-
ology are firms which weave polypropylene tufted carpet
backing and bags on wide looms designed for this purpose, and
which in a number of cases also extrude polypropylene in tape
form from granules or chips supplied by the petrochemical
industry. It should not be forgotten that such firms may also
continue to spin and weave jute. Some of the Innovators did
in fact cease jute spinning and weaving shortly after making a
major investment in polypropylene extrusion and weaving. Low
& Bonar is the best example of this. Other Innovators, however, such as Don Bros. Buist and Scott & Robertson, continue
to spin and weave jute as well as extruding and weaving polypropylene. Such businesses, therefore, continue to compete
against the Traditionalists above; the former usually having
much more sophisticated jute operations, and therefore limiting the scope for survival of the latter.

Under the heading of Reorientation have been placed the
smaller firm of Craiks of Forfar, and also half of the strategy of Sidlaw Industries. These two firms have spent considerable efforts in entering the market for Hessian wallcoverings.
In the case of Sidlaw the sum is estimated at around £2m. over
the five years to 1977. This involves making a fairly high
quality of cloth for use as a wallcovering, either in its
natural or "loomstate" form, or following the application of

a pattern or dye. This is a market where jute has taken over
from flax on the basis of price; and in general the appeal of
Hessian wallcoverings is based upon cheapness and the fashion
element of a natural fibre. So far as the jute manufacturers
are concerned, this market has two significant characteristics.
First, the product is very largely sold loomstate in a variety
of possible patterns to the laminator firms who may themselves
introduce further pattern effects into the product so that the
final nature of the goods is not in the hands of the jute firms
themselves. Second, although the market for the goods has expanded considerably over the past four or five years, it is
overwhelmingly an export one (to Europe and the U.S.) with all
the attendant risks of fashion change and dependence upon the
external value of Sterling.

Diversification, as the term is used in Tables 3.1 and 3.2, has
been a strategy adopted by two firms, Thomson Shepherd and
Caird (Dundee), both having used their previous experience of
spinning or weaving jute for the carpet trade to move into wov-
en and tufted carpets, the other eventually into tufted carpet
manufacturing. In both of these cases the firms appear to
have acknowledged that competition was too great in the traditional jute market, that economic forces appeared to favour
the continued survival in the traditional market of the large
firms rather than smaller concerns, and that carpet manufacture
or printing represented a means of survival involving relatively limited capital outlay and again a limited amount of new
technology.

Into our category of Conglomeration fall one small firm and
part of Sidlaw's strategy. Again it is worth repeating here
that there is an element of judgement involved in placing companies into the various categories, and conceivably other
firms could have been classed as Conglomerates. Low & Bonar,
for example, has had a significant electrical engineering subsidiary (Bonar Long) since the immediate post-war period, and
has recently developed its own floorcovering interests (Flotex). The predominant feature of the group has, however, been
innovation through Polytape in polypropylene extrusion and
S.F.S. in tape weaving. H. & A. Scott, likewise, has an
engineering subsidiary, Lomax & Smith; but again the dominant
feature of the firm's strategy has been polypropylene extrusion
and tape weaving. Thus Sidlaw and Malcolm, Ogilvie have been
formally categorised as Conglomerates because the expansion of
their interests unrelated to industrial textiles has been a
significant and characteristic part of their strategy for survival. In the case of Sidlaw (detailed below) this has taken
the firm into hardware wholesaling and operations ancillary to
North Sea oil exploration and drilling (another area in which

Low & Bonar also have interests). As regards Malcolm,
Ogilvie, which in 1968 had fewer than 500 employees, although
diversified interests (basically Fibro spinning) have not been
totally successful, the "conglomeration" into continuous casting of high quality bronze alloy, begun in the early 1960's,
has taken over from the company's jute interests with much
success. In both of these cases the firms appear to have been
prepared to branch out into markets quite unrelated to textiles;
and it is interesting that such a policy has been followed by
two firms at the opposite ends of the size spectrum within the
group of traditional jute manufacturers.

In Chapter 2 it was noted that firms in the market covered by
this study had died either as a result of being acquired by
competitors or simply through closing down from a lack of
traditional jute spinning or weaving business. This process
halved the number of independent businesses formally in the
industry in the decade from 1966-1976. This chapter concentrates upon the surviving firms, and in this section a general
view has been presented of how firms used the strategies of
diversification for survival. That the adoption of some
strategy was essential may be seen if one is reminded of the
decline of the industry up to 1977. Taking 1967 as a base
year (100), output of yarn and of cloth had fallen by 1977 to
index levels of 41.1 and 21.4 respectively, employment on a
similar basis had fallen to 52.3 (although, as noted earlier
in Chapter 2, the employment statistics probably underestimate
the decline in the market), and the number of firms in the
industry had (by our formal measure) fallen by 53%.

The predominant response of the surviving firms has been fully
to adopt polypropylene technology, although it should again be
emphasised that this had not precluded some firms from continuing with jute spinning and weaving at the same time. Nor has
it precluded such firms from spinning other fibres such as
nylon or rayon, or having some non-textile operations. Innovation has fortunately been a strategy open to firms of
markedly different size. There appears to have been no
particular entry barrier to the new market either in terms of
large initial capital expenditure, nor in the form of loss of
economies of scale by operating with a small number of looms
for tape weaving, or "lines" for extruding. (The formal statistical relationship between firm size and growth is examined
in Chapter 4). It may then be asked why the other firms in
the industry did not follow a path of "innovation"; and this
question should be applied both for surviving firms and to those
which died. With regard to non-surviving firms, much of the
answer to the question lies in individual, often family, circumstances. As mentioned in Chapter 2, the majority of the

firms which failed to survive the 1960's were small, family
owned/managed, non-integrated weaving concerns. Their market
for tufted carpet backing and packaging disappeared so quickly
to polypropylene at the end of that decade that a very rapid
decision was forced upon them. To many, the untried technology involved and additional finance required for entry into
polypropylene may have appeared as considerable barriers.
Coinciding as these issues did for some firms with additional
problems of family succession, such factors may simply have
hastened an already largely inevitable decision to terminate
the business operations. Among surviving firms, entry into
polypropylene was rejected for more positive reasons; although among the firms classed above as Traditionalists (and
even the single Hesitant) one either has to recognise except-
ional circumstances or to regard the current survival as
temporary rather than long-term. Those firms which have chosen
a strategy of reorientation, diversification or conglomeration
have rejected polypropylene either because there have been
forces in their background pulling in another direction
(Thomson, Shepherd, for example, had a strong carpet background
having been one of the original jute carpet manufacturers),
because they felt that they had a special advantage in relation
to a unique product (as in Caird's space-dyeing operations, or
Malcolm, Ogilvie's continuous bronze casting), or because they
felt that by the early 1970's manufacturing capacity in polypropylene tape weaving was becoming almost excessive relative
to carpet backing and other demand.

Thus an account of the strategy of diversification across the
industry as a whole reveals a situation where, although most
firms embraced the new polypropylene technology wholeheartedly,
other directions for diversification were found, and where
some continuing firms have so far avoided diversification
altogether. In the following section a series of short case
histories is presented whose aim is to allow one further to
analyse the economic process of diversification, and, together with the results of the statistical analysis below, to
enable one to arrive at more detailed conclusions in the final
section of this chapter.

            CASE HISTORIES

Although the diversification of jute firms is often thought of
as being a fairly recent phenomenon, some firms were clearly
anticipating a declining future for jute even in the mid
1950's. Leveson's data (Leveson, 1973) indicate the results
of earlier policies. The chairman of Low and Bonar warned in
1956 (Low & Bonar, 1955 Annual Report):

"During the past year it has become clear that
at present price levels in the U.K. jute's
position as a packaging material for certain
commodities is being more and more challenged
by competition from substitutes such as paper
and from bulk handling. ... Spinners in the
United Kingdom ... are now faced with having
to fight off the competition of substitutes
by ever-increasing cuts in profit margins, and
possibly even by cutting into actual production
costs."

Among the smaller companies at this time, Caird (Dundee), for
example, recognised (Caird (Dundee), 1957 Annual Report) that
its acquisition of James Prain constituted a valuable non-
jute expansion in the current climate.

What these examples indicate is that the recognition of a need
to diversify away from an undue dependence upon traditional
jute end-use markets was something which had existed for some
time in the Dundee industry prior to the late 1960's. It is
also a reminder of the fact that diversification of a kind had
been going on over this period insofar as Dundee firms had
left the cruder jute markets for sacking and packaging (which
Jute Control was gradually opening up to Indian competition
throughout the 1960's) and were concentrating upon woven carpet
backing by the mid 1960's - the latter market being in its
early years largely an export one to the United States. It
was the rapidity of the loss of the tufted carpet backing
market to polypropylene in the late 1960's which introduced
the need for a much wider strategy of diversification; and
it is upon this wider strategy that the analysis in the case
histories concentrates. What this section does is to trace
the history of diversification in some of the individual
firms, and note the motivation, direction and success or otherwise of such a strategy in individual cases.

<u>Low & Bonar Group</u>

The experience of Low & Bonar exemplifies many of the issues
in this area. On the one hand it appears to have been quite
far-sighted in recognising the need for moving away from
dependence upon jute. On the other, the firm does not always
appear to have fully anticipated the "teething" problems of
entering new markets and adopting new technologies.
Frequently there appear to have been delays in bringing new
plant into operation. A final problem faced by many diversifiers was that of moving into a new market area only to find
competition there much more severe than anticipated; and in

some cases this type of situation was aggravated by a cyclical downturn in demand for such products.

Low & Bonar's diversification has involved the development of new fibres and fabrics in packaging, and also operations in engineering. Thus in the mid 1950's it developed a plastic proofed tarpauling - Flaxtite - and also entered into a joint venture to produce transparent packaging made of cellulose film. These policies continued through the development of more sophisticated heavy-gauge polythene sacks - Lobosacks - and by the late 1960's into polypropylene and the company's new product, Flotex - a synthetic floorcovering produced through electrostatic flocking. A further point which particularly distinguishes Low & Bonar from other firms in the Dundee industrial textiles industry is that its Dundee activities are only a very small part of its total spread of interests. At the time of writing up this study in 1981, of the Group's total of some 9,000 employees, only 5,500 (61%) were employed in the U.K., and only about 1,200 (13%) in the Dundee area. Comparing developments over our period of major interest, in 1967 25.5% of earnings were generated by engineering activities, both in the U.K. and Africa, and of the textiles and packaging earnings which constituted 67.9% of the total, 74.7% came from Canada and Africa (Low & Bonar, 1969 Annual Report). In 1977, textiles and packaging still accounted for 72.1% of total Group earnings, and these total earnings continued overwhelmingly to come from abroad - 51.1% from Africa, 19.2% from Canada, and the remainder from the U.K. and the other countries of the E.E.C. (Low & Bonar, 1977 Annual Report).

With regard to product markets the Group's major non-engineering diversification venture has of course been that of polypropylene. Low & Bonar commenced production in 1969 on the basis of two subsidiary companies jointly held with Sidlaw Industries (which in 1977 sold its share to Low & Bonar which then became the sole owner of the two firms). The principal market, to begin with, was tufted carpet primary backing. Since then, however, the Group's subsidiaries Polytape and Synthetic Fabrics (Scotland), operating respectively as extruders and tape weavers, have expanded into other markets for polypropylene. A distinguishing feature of Low & Bonar, however, has been its additional interest in engineering. After World War II the company acquired a controlling interest in Bonar, Long - a transformer manufacturer; and by the mid 1950's had pushed further in this direction by the formation of Sturrock Power Installations in the electrical contracting field, and through Bonar, Long's expansion into switchgear and, later, capacitors. The latest developments in this general area have included the formation of component

engineering subsidiaries both to service Bonar, Long and to
sell outside the Group (Dudhope Engineering, Logan Engineering,
and Haddingtonshire Fabricators), and also the establishment
of a service company for North Sea oil exploration and drilling
operations. In addition to these the company also has its own
subsidiary for producing printing cylinders for the packaging
market - Gravure Cylinders. This last company also sells to
outside customers. By the end of our period of study the
company had, however, sold its smaller local engineering subsidiaries Dudhope, Logan and Sturrock; and Low & Bonar's
newer engineering acquisitions such as the G.H.P. group of
companies and its purchase of Bibby & Baron in the field of
paper products and other containers illustrate its strategy of
acquiring larger, more diverse U.K. businesses outwith the
Dundee area in addition to its policy of continued expansion
in engineering and textiles overseas.

Low & Bonar's diversification has not, however, been without
its problems. In engineering in particular the problem has
been that of operating in markets where output has been subject
to a cyclical pattern of demand. In the case of transformers,
for example, home new orders rose from around £33m. in 1959 to
a peak of almost £70m. in 1963, and then fell again to under
£45m. in 1968. The result of this was severe competition and
low prices in the late 1950's and very early 1960's, an expansion of earnings up to about 1964, and a subsequent downturn of profits and prices. Thus although Bonar, Long's pre-
tax profits expanded from £163,222 in 1959 to £671,007 in 1963,
the years which followed witnessed, in the words of successive
Annual Reports, "very intensive competition and depressed
prices", "minimal profit margins", and again prices which were
"wretchedly low". Some idea of the impact of this swing over
the 1960's may be gained from the following data which apply
to its operations worldwide.

TABLE 3.3   Low & Bonar Ltd.: Share of "Engineering" in Pre-
            tax Earnings (%)

1960	10.7	1965	27.5
1961	23.7	1966	27.0
1962	27.0	1967	25.5
1963	40.4	1968	10.2
1964	38.9	1969	(7.6) i.e. loss

Source: Annual Reports & Accounts

To some extent the Group has suffered similarly in the field
of transparent packaging. Here the firm met increased competition and narrowing profit margins in the early years of its

expansion into this market; and competition appears to have
remained keen throughout the 1960's. Again, as in the case
of jute and heavy electrical equipment, demand for packaging,
being a derived demand, is heavily dependent upon the general
climate of demand in the economy and, in the case of packaging,
on the volume of international trade. Thus the packaging
subsidiaries' results during the 1970's were disappointing;
and the Group's expansion in this area has most recently been
by way of acquisition - through the purchase of Bibby & Baron
(Holdings) in 1976.

TABLE 3.4   Low & Bonar Ltd.: Share of "Packaging" in Pretax
            Earnings (%)

1973	46.5	1975	31.5	1977	23.3
1964	66.3	1976	26.5		

Source: as in Table 3.3

The other characteristic of diversification apparent from Low
& Bonar's experience is the longer-than-expected time scale
involved in bringing some diversification projects on stream.
Such new operations often appear, in addition, to have taken
longer than anticipated originally to make a contribution to
the company's profits. This latter phenomenon is possibly due
to the former plus the adoption of a "conservative" depreciation policy in respect of risky capital-intensive projects.
It may be claimed that this is a phenomenon well recognised
in business circles, and that "outsiders" adopt an un-
realistically short time horizon in expecting new business
ventures to generate returns. Indeed the chairman of Low &
Bonar warned shareholders in 1955 that "New developments and
new businesses do not become worthwhile profit-earners over-
night". As an example, the transparent packaging interests
of the company in the mid 1950's seem to have encountered
technical difficulties as well as poor prices before making
a contribution to profits. More recently the company's Flotex project, which began production in 1974, had not by 1977
contributed any profits to the Group. The company earlier
admitted in the case of polypropylene that "a good deal of
know-how and technical expertise are required to produce a
suitable fabric"; but Flotex appears to have presented more
intractable problems. Thus, in addition to the inevitable
starting losses in 1972, the company admitted in 1973 that
"teething troubles ... were taking longer than had been anticipated"; and despite progress in 1974 (Flotex was still
making losses), 1975 was a year in which this division
"experienced serious technical problems". In 1976 losses
approached £½m. on a turnover of just over £2m., while in

1977 sales increased by about 10% but losses remained at
around 1976 levels.

Sidlaw Industries

Low & Bonar's experience has been dealt with at some length
because it represents not only a more complex form of diversification in the industry, but also because it highlights some
of the significant problems for firms in this policy area.
The other major company in the market - Sidlaw Industries -
has on the face of things pursued a more cautious and limited
policy of diversification. This company continued for some
time into the 1960's to base its activities upon jute; and
some 60% of output was geared to floorcovering markets. This
involved both jute yarn and cloth for carpets and linoleum.
Thus despite isolated references in its Annual Reports to the
possibility of using spare factory capacity for non-jute goods,
the firm continued to demonstrate its faith in its traditional
market by re-equipment with technologically advanced jute
plant. Even by the early 1970's the company's view (Dundee
Chamber Journal, September 1971, p.585) was that it intended
to remain "pre-eminent within the jute industry"; and on this
basis was still looking forward (Sidlaw Industries, 1971
Annual Report) to "being able to maintain a profitable jute
manufacturing activity for some years ahead".

Nonetheless the need to plan for a future in which jute faced
a declining demand from traditional users seems to have been
something of which Sidlaw was aware, according to discussions
with senior executives. Indeed, at one stage a full-time
director was appointed with the sole remit of seeking out
appropriate acquisitions; and an American consultant was
employed for a similar purpose. As the senior management
viewed the position, Sidlaw had only a limited range of
options open to it. Acquisition of some of the more efficient
of its smaller competitors was on the face of it attractive as
a short-term proposition, and was indeed, as noted in Chapter
2, implemented to a small extent. But this was not regarded
as a long-term solution; and even in the shorter term was
felt likely to raise the question of monopoly power in the
industry, with a possible response from the Monopolies and
Mergers Commission. Other options considered were those of
investing abroad, or of integrating forward into carpet manufacture. The latter was, however, rejected on the grounds
that existing customers would have been antagonised: a very
large part of Sidlaw's yarn and cloth output was already going
into woven and tufted carpets by the mid 1960's. It must also
have been recognised that to the extent that the ups and downs
of the jute industry's fortunes during the 1960's had largely

been those of the floorcoverings market, there would be no
escape from these through integrating into a section of the
floorcoverings market itself.

Despite the above reasoning, Sidlaw's major diversification
at the end of the 1960's was into the closely related polypropylene field; and it was achieved by taking an equal share
with Low & Bonar in Polytape and S.F.S. These developments
were initially on a fairly small scale. By the end of the
1960's less than £½m. had been committed - and more than two-
thirds of the company's turnover and profits still at this time
came from U.K. spinning and weaving of jute.

In addition to its investment in polypropylene, Sidlaw, from
the late 1960's onwards, acquired facilities for manufacturing
other man-made fibres. These were predominantly rayon and
nylon, and were designed to serve the markets for tufted carpet
face yarns and children's clothing. The final stage of Sidlaw's diversification programme (coming with the accession of
Sir John Carmichael to the chairmanship of the company in 1970)
has seen the farthest spreading of the firm's interests from
its traditional jute base. In 1972 the company acquired both a
hardware wholesaling concern (P. & R. Fleming), and also a stake
in the North Sea oil servicing industry through the acquisition
of Aberdeen Service Co. (North Sea). Nonetheless the former
venture cost £506,000 and the later £72,000, compared with the
expenditure of £1.5m. the same year in respect of South Mills
(Textiles), although one has to bear in mind that subsequent to
its non-textile acquisitions Sidlaw invested considerable sums
in its Fleming and North Sea oil interests. Sidlaw's non-
textile ventures have within the period of our study represented
a small part of the company's expansion strategy; and while it
may be suggested that P. & R. Fleming carried out a "merchanting"
function with which Sidlaw was familiar through its jute operations, one senior executive at Sidlaw frankly admitted that the
Aberdeen Service Co. venture was "a step in the dark".

From 1970 onwards as Sidlaw began to reduce its dependence upon
jute the firm entered into a situation in which it was faced
with poorer returns on its traditional base in jute while not
yet reaping the full rewards of its diversified investment.
Speaking of the position in the early 1970's the chairman
commented (Sidlaw Industries, 1971 Annual Report):

> "The Company is in a difficult state of trans-
> ition. On the one hand, it is not easy to earn
> a satisfactory level of profits on jute manu-
> facturing when competitive products are becoming
> increasingly penetrative because of price

> advantages. On the other hand, profits from
> the expansion of other activities and entry
> into new activities have to bear not only
> development charges but also finance charges
> until new installations become commissioned
> and profitable."

Sidlaw's diversification policy appears to have been less consistent than that of other firms. At first, apart from its
Polytape and S.F.S. partnerships with Low & Bonar, Sidlaw
appears to have pursued a diversification policy of finding
new markets for existing products - for example Hessian wallcoverings. This may be contrasted with Low & Bonar's policy
of adopting new technologies for satisfying existing markets
(paper, polythene and polypropylene in the container area,
and polypropylene and Flotex in floorcoverings). Emphasising
this policy contrast, Sidlaw in 1977 withdrew from Polytape
and S.F.S. in recognition of the disparate textile interests
in which the firm was by then engaged, and in order to provide
finance for other areas of diversification. As events have
turned out, Sidlaw has more recently sold off its hardware
wholesaling interests, withdrawn from the Hessian wallcoverings
markets, and has been forced by lack of demand to close down
significant parts of its jute spinning capacity. The firm has
thus doubled back on its earlier policy of seeking new market
areas for jute, and has most recently sought to participate in
the oil-related prosperity of north-east Scotland, not only
directly through Aberdeen Service Co. but also through "associate" investments in offshore supplies, hotel services and
property development (Seaforth Maritime, and Grampian Land).
Sidlaw is an example, therefore, of a business which has
diversified on a rather cautious basis. It has frequently
sought to remain close to its textiles/carpeting base; it has
expanded largely by acquisition; and some of its diversified
enterprises appear to be operated on a "portfolio" basis
rather than incorporated into the main business.

Caird (Dundee)

Some of the smaller businesses among our group of firms have
followed a different path of diversification, and have moved
with success away from their original dependence upon jute
spinning and weaving into totally new areas associated with
man-made fibres. Caird (Dundee), for example, moved into
rayon spinning in the mid 1950's, beginning with the acquisition of James Prain; and although there appear to have been
initial difficulties with new equipment, the company continued to pursue a policy of reducing its dependence upon jute,
which it recognised could not compete on a price basis with

new synthetic packaging materials,and the use of synthetics
in other traditional jute end-use areas. The problems of the
decline in demand for jute were aggravated in this case by
Caird's having committed itself after 1945 almost exclusively
to the linoleum industry. Considerable capital investment had
been made in the immediate post-war period in broad looms, and
the company had a large share of the market for quality backing
for linoleum. Thus in the 1960's in addition to cutting back
its hessian output in adjustment to the rapid decline in demand
for linoleum backing, and producing wider cloths for tufted
carpet backing, the firm significantly enlarged its synthetic
fibre blending and spinning capacity geared towards the production of carpet pile yarn. Caird, in common with other
firms in the market, entered the polypropylene market in the
late 1960's - in this case through a joint venture with Smith
& Nephew, initially geared to sack and bag production. In the
first instance Caird was in fact merely selling bags and sacking
made from Smith & Nephew polypropylene.

However, a distinguishing feature of Caird's diversification
programme was that in the long term it chose not to rely upon
polypropylene or other synthetic fibres in a direct sense.
Indeed although, as mentioned earlier, one of the attractions
of the James Prain acquisition of 1956 was the synthetic yarn
capacity of the latter, production of this yarn ceased at the
end of 1971, only 18 months after the firm had closed its jute
works. Caird's new policy involved working on a commission
basis for carpet manufacturers, initially in the space dyeing
of yarns which enabled tufted carpet manufacturers to produce
a colour finish similar to popular woven carpets, and latterly
through tufted carpet printing - again initially on a commission basis. Space dyeing involves the application of various
colours to a nylon yarn which has first been knitted into a
tubular fabric. This "sock" passes through the various
dyeing processes which ensure that the dyes are applied and
sealed on to the material. Once these processes have been
completed, the tubular sock is deknitted or rattled down and
wound on to cones which become the basic raw material for
tufted carpet manufacture. The effect of tufting with space-
dyed yarns is to produce a carpet with semi-random elements.
Prior to the advent of carpet printing, this was a very
popular style of carpet on the Continent, and some 90% of
Caird's output was for Continental tufters. Carpet printing
involves printing a pattern on to a "white" tufted carpet.
The dyes are applied by a series of tubular rollers, each
containing a different colour and contributing a separate
section of the pattern. The tufted material passes round
four to twelve rollers which apply the colours. These dyes
are then fixed on to the material by chemical processes,

after which the carpet is washed and dried before it is completed by the application of a secondary backing.

The space dyeing project began in 1969 with a capital investment of £500,000, and additional systems were installed in
1971 and 1972. But in common with other firms' experiences
of diversification, this did not prove to be an immediate
panacea for the company's ills. Despite the chairman being
able to report in 1968 that "non-jute interests now form a
substantial part of our business", a sterner warning about undue optimism was delivered to shareholders the following year
(Caird (Dundee), 1969 Annual Report).

> "Rumours were circulating earlier in the year
> about the enormous potential of the space
> dyeing development, which it was suggested
> would transform the company's fortunes in a
> relatively short period. I think it is only
> right, therefore, that I should put this in
> its proper perspective. I would remind share-
> holders that your company is still primarily
> a jute manufacturing company and that the
> greater part of both the fixed and current
> assets are invested in this activity. While
> the newer developments, i.e. Polyweave, the
> spinning of synthetic fibres and space dyeing
> will represent an increasing proportion of
> the turnover in the future the limited capital
> available for their development will inevit-
> ably mean that it will be some time before
> they can grow to the extent necessary to
> carry the bulk of the overhead expenses and
> adequately remunerate the company's capital.
> We have no option, therefore, but to continue
> to be primarily a jute company for some time
> ahead and this is bound to be reflected in our
> profits."

In fact the company suffered over this period from a downturn
in demand for tufted carpets, from technical problems in
bringing into operation space dyeing equipment, and competition in building up sales of polypropylene products. Rationalisation resulted in the company sinking the largest part of
its resources into space dyeing - this venture constituting
"by far the most important of our activities" according to
the chairman in 1971; and by the early 1970's the firm had
invested some £1.5m. in space dyeing, had sold off its polypropylene interests, closed down its synthetic yarn spinning
plant, and terminated its jute commitment.

However, 1973 saw the beginning of the second phase of Caird's
expansion - tufted carpet printing. Caird realised that it
had somewhat saturated the space dyeing market, and that carpet printing was in any case taking over from the space dyeing
of carpet yarns. With space dyeing operations working at only
two-thirds of capacity, the firm invested heavily in carpet
printing plant - about £2.5m. having been spent in the first
half of the 1970's. Developments over the past few years have
continued to favour the carpet printing side of the business,
and a natural expansion of this has been to move into carpet
tufting. The final move into carpet backing (i.e. secondary
backing with foam) was begun in 1976; and this, of course,
brought the company back into closer contact with a business
which it had left almost a decade previously. This latest
phase of Caird's development of becoming a carpet manufacturer
in its own right has been encouraged by the high transport
costs of its U.K. and international customers in sending
"white" tufted carpet to Caird for printing and return. The
company thus expanded initially into offering a tufting
service, and in 1976 installed carpet backing capacity - still
operating on a commission basis. One interesting further
development of Caird's new total involvement in carpet manufacture is that carpet wholesalers can commission the firm to
supply carpets to their specific requirements; and it has been
suggested that this provides wholesalers with a product at much
lower cost. Caird also sells a limited amount of its output
through its own shops, and has added to its carpet range in
recent years by using the weft laying process to produce shag-
pile carpets.

The case of Caird (Dundee) illustrates a number of interesting
phenomena. First, the firm has gone through a series of stages
in its diversification strategy. From a total dependence upon
jute, the firm added synthetic pile yarn spinning and polypropylene weaving in the 1950's and 1960's respectively. These,
however, together with jute, were phased out by the early
1970's. Space dyeing was invested in heavily in the early
1970's, but suffered from problems of over-capacity in the
market as a whole and rapid market and technical obsolescence
as carpet printing became a technically feasible way of satisfying changing tastes in the carpet market. The latest phase
of investment (carpet printing), begun in 1973, was therefore
necessary; and a final development, again caused by competition and capacity problems, has been vertical integration into
tufting and backing, and to a minor extent forward into carpet
retailing, with the result that the firm is now essentially a
carpet manufacturer. Some indication of the phasing out of
old interests and the introduction of new ventures can be
gained from the following data.

TABLE 3.5   Caird (Dundee) Ltd.: Disaggregated Annual Output

	Jute ('000 tons)	Space Dyeing ('000 tons)	Carpet Printing ('000 sq.yds.)
1964	13.4	-	-
1965	14.5	-	-
1966	12.8	-	-
1967	7.8	-	-
1968	6.9	-	-
1969	6.1	-	-
1970	1.0	0.8	-
1971	-	2.5	-
1972	-	4.6	-
1973	-	5.7	479
1974	-	4.9	2,191
1975	-	3.4	3,444

Source :   calculated from graphs in Manson, J. (1976). The Major Changes Undertaken by Caird (Dundee) Ltd. in their Diversification. Unpublished D.M.S. Dissertation, Dundee College of Technology.

Second, Caird has exhibited financial and technical problems of diversification. The company found difficulty in raising the sums necessary to finance the space dyeing project of the late 1960's; and delays occurred in implementing the carpet printing project until sufficient profits had been generated from the dyeing operations to fund it. Like other firms too, the process of implementing new projects was not without its technical problems. Manson (1976) speaks of such ventures "not (being) accomplished without many teething troubles". Specifically with regard to its new ventures in the 1970's, the company (Caird (Dundee), 1970 Annual Report) found that the space dyeing operation "had taken longer than we anticipated to build up"; and in respect of carpet printing (Caird (Dundee), 1973 Annual Report) that "the operation of a plant of this type calls for a high degree of skill and expertise and the running in period can be costly and can last for a considerable time".

Scott & Robertson

A roughly similar history, so far as reduced dependence upon the jute industry is concerned, was experienced by Scott & Robertson - the result of a merger in 1965 between James Scott & Sons and Robertson Industrial Textiles. By the time of the merger the group had already moved into paper packaging as well as the spinning of man-made fibres, in addition to its traditional linoleum backing and broad-loom jute interests.

The jute interests were very largely geared to tufted carpet
backing and linoleum hessian, although circular loom capacity
was devoted to sack manufacture. By the late 1960's and early
1970's the firm was moving into new fibres: recognising, in the
chairman's own words (Scott & Robertson, 1970 Annual Report),
"the limitations and difficulties which bear upon the jute producing industry". In fact the following year saw the closure of
part of the group's jute weaving capacity, and a further exten-
sion of the company's man-made fibre activities. The company
has nonetheless maintained a presence in the jute industry
through woven carpet yarn spinning and some jute weaving, mainly
for roofing felt backing - the chairman commenting in 1973 (Scott
& Robertson, 1973 Annual Report) that "we have every intention of
continuing our jute manufacturing business. I believe that despite the changes which have taken place in the whole reformation
of the jute industry in Dundee, there will be left a reduced
but viable and profitable trade". The company has, however,
continued to expand its commitment to man-made fibres - in
common with other firms in the industry establishing subsidiaries
outwith the Dundee area nearer major markets. Again in common
with other businesses which have diversified into new technology,
Scott & Robertson's new ventures have not been without their
teething problems. One Annual Report (Scott & Robertson, 1975)
speaks of the effectiveness of expanded operations being
"severely impaired by a number of mechanical and design faults
in the new plant". The company now, however, appears to have
achieved a desired balance between its traditional fibre markets
and those based upon new technologies.

Thomson Shepherd & Co.

As a final example of individual-company strategy one may take
a less obviously successful case of diversification, where the
company has been acquired by a large international non-textile
firm. Thomson Shepherd, which in 1946 added rayon spinning to
its predominantly jute carpet business, ceased manufacturing
furnishing fabrics in the mid 1950's, and by 1965 had also
ceased production of jute carpets after "heavy losses". The
firm's other interests at this time continued to be the
spinning of jute yarn, and Fibro (rayon) spinning - the latter
based upon raw material from Courtaulds. With the decline in
its jute carpet business the company established an engineering
subsidiary. Bristol Tool & Gauge (Scotland) Ltd. was bought
in 1960 and renamed Seafield Tool & Gauge after the location
of the firm's main works. At the same time the company moved
into wool carpet manufacture. Production of quality Wiltons
began in 1958, and the acquisition of Darville Carpets of
Monifieth in 1961 added Axminster to the company's range.

The company's strategy was at that time based upon three broad interests: yarn spinning - Fibro and jute; carpets - jute initially, and wool at a later date; and engineering - Seafield was added to by Dundee Metal Spraying Co. in 1967. In carpets and yarn the company suffered from lack of size and an inability to enter the man-made fibre industry on a sufficiently large scale. For example, in 1970 it lost a regular Ministry of Defence contract for its own carpets because of the adoption by the Ministry of new contract procedures favouring large firms. The company estimated that at that time the loss cost it some 15-20% of its carpet turnover. In the late 1960's the firm suffered from a downturn in woven carpets which affected its own woollen sales and also demand for jute yarn for woven carpet backing; and in 1972 the firm closed down its viscose rayon spinning unit on the grounds that it was being operated on too small a scale to be profitable. These factors, together with an unfortunate bringing on stream of new texile plant in 1967 just as demand in its various markets was falling off, contributed to poor profits.

Finally, the company's diversification into engineering failed because of an overdependence upon subcontracted jobs. In the late 1960's some customers were lost through bankruptcy as the general level of engineering activity fell; and other customers began taking work back into their own shops which had previously been subcontracted to Seafield. The engineering subsidiaries were thus closed down in 1971, the company having realised, in its own words (Thomson Shepherd, 1971 Annual Report), that "instead of acting as an insurance against decline in our other activities, they had become a liability". The company then decided to concentrate its efforts largely in woven and tufted carpets, and has recently increased tufted carpet making capacity significantly.

Although the original firm has lost its corporate independence, the case of Thomson Shepherd illustrates both the difficulties and the capacity for survival of smaller businesses in this market. Thus the company has suffered on a number of occasions from its relatively small scale of operations - the firm employed an average of fewer than 500 people over the period 1967-1977. In high quality jute yarn spinning, for example, although the firm was at one time one of the three or four largest producers, its costs were higher than those of competitors because of the incidence of largely fixed expenses of quality control etc. spread over a smaller output. In these circumstances the company decided that rather than re-equip its jute spinning operations when the need arose it would buy in its jute yarn requirements for its own woven

carpet production, and the firm ceased jute spinning in 1975.
On the other hand, even as an essentially family business,
Thomson Shepherd invested considerable sums of money in new
equipment during its various phases of development. This
included re-equipment with broad looms for woven wool carpet
production in the early 1960's, and considerable investment
in tufting capacity in the mid 1970's. The company has also
maintained its position in the market by virtue of a very high
level of design and technical performance, including the
production of two-pile-height multicolour Axminister carpets,
and the creation of particular designs on tufted carpets by
the use of computer-controlled tufting machines which produce
a "woven carpet" appearance at a much lower cost than competing products.

STATISTICAL TESTS ON DIVERSIFICATION

Earlier sections of this chapter analysed the conduct or behaviour of firms in the Dundee jute industry in terms of their
diversification strategy in largely descriptive terms. Thus
an analysis has been offered at an aggregated level of the
extent and directions of diversification among the 17 surviving firms in the industry over the period 1965-1977 (Tables
3.1 and 3.2 above); and individual case studies of patterns
of diversification within single firms have also been reported.
In this section it is intended to use the knowledge of the
firms' diversification policies (by interviews with senior
management in the businesses concerned, as well as by reference to other sources and journal articles) to analyse the
impact of diversification at a statistical level.

The first requirement for this analysis was to produce two
groups of firms, referred to as Diversified and Non-diversified. It has to be accepted that the basis of classification
here is subjective and impressionistic rather than one which
is statistically validated. The relevant factors involved in
the classification are the extent of non-jute interests, the
extent to which firms have adopted new technologies (and so
entered new end-use markets), and the relatedness or otherwise of new markets to traditional ones. Taking these
criteria, the following classification was adopted. This
produces a categorisation of 8 Diversified and 7 Non-diversified companies, comprising those 15 firms for whom the
necessary information was available over the period 1967-1977.

TABLE 3.6   Classification of Firms for Analysis of
                       Diversification

Diversified	Non-diversified
Caird (Dundee)	Buist Spinning Co.
Don Bros. Buist	Craiks
Wm. Halley	Hardie & Smith
Low & Bonar	Sidlaw
Malcolm Ogilvie	Thos. Thomson
H. & A. Scott	Thomson Shepherd
Scott & Fyfe	J. & D. Wilkie
Scott & Robertson	

The next part of the analysis involves deciding what it is
that one expects diversified firms to achieve which would
distinguish their performance from that of non-diversified
firms.   Three areas of performance are specified which permit
of statistical analysis.

1. Profitability levels (average over 10 years)
2. Profit variability over 10-year period
3. Growth of assets, sales and employment.

The a priori assumption is that diversified firms would have
enjoyed higher average profits than non-diversified firms, or
would at least have maintained their earlier level of profits.
It is also assumed that the variability of rates of return on
capital employed over time would be lower for diversified than
for non-diversified firms.   Finally, it is assumed that the
growth rates (of assets, sales or employment) for diversified
firms would be higher than in respect of non-diversified firms.
The likely relationship between diversification and growth is
complex.   Growth may lead to or cause diversification.   That
is, diversification may be a function of growth, in the sense
that firms with growth ambitions may prefer to or have to
satisfy these in markets beyond their primary base if to
expand in this base market would lead to serious competition
with existing market rivals.   A strategy of diversification
would be even more imperative here if the primary market is a
static or declining one, as is the case in the particular
market studied here.   Diversification, however, may also facil-
itate growth.   That is, achieved growth may be a function of
the existing extent of diversification if diversified enterprises are exempt from the existing market bounds to growth
mentioned immediately above.   In each case the relationship
between growth and diversification is assumed to be positive,
and this is the finding of a number of U.K. studies.   It is
the causal link which is uncertain.

In the following tests profit rates are measured relative to
the U.K. manufacturing industries average in any year, and
growth rates are measured in real terms by reference to
appropriate price indices. The first test comprised a simple
comparison of means of the various measures, distinguishing
between the two categories of firms, and applying a one-tailed
t test in the a priori predicted direction. Because of the
incidence of losses and negative growth rates arithmetic rather
than geometric means were used. The results were as follows.

TABLE 3.7   Analysis of Mean Performance of Diversified and
            Non-diversified Firms

		Diversified (8)	Non-Diversified (7)	t
i.	Mean profit ratio 1968-77 (%)	11.7	7.1	1.0455
	Standard deviation	6.1	9.5	
ii.	Mean profit ratio 1971-77/1968-70	1.344	1.672	0.4706
	Standard deviation	1.124	1.387	
iii.	Average profit variability (residual variance around linear trend) 1968-77	41.8821	130.3715	1.4409*
	Standard deviation	36.7001	156.8743	
iv.	Average coefficient of variation of profit ratios 1968-77	66.5	81.2	0.5385
	Standard deviation	55.9	40.0	
v.	Mean annual asset growth rate 1968-77	1.9	-6.5	1.9091**
	Standard deviation	8.5	7.3	
vi.	Mean annual sales growth rate 1968-77	2.4	-1.2	1.1250
	Standard deviation	6.0	5.3	
vii.	Mean annual employment growth rate 1968-77	-0.7	-4.2	1.1290
	Standard deviation	6.3	4.8	
viii.	Mean opening size: Assets (£'000 1967)	2,881	1,461	0.6320
	Standard deviation	4,924	2,703	
	Sales (£'000 1967)	6,155	3,002	0.7146
	Standard deviation	9,406	5,820	

TABLE 3.7 (cont'd)

	Diversified (8)	Non-Diversified (7)	t
Employment (number 1968)	1,098	1,008	0.1119
Standard deviation	1,021	1,813	
ix. Mean income per employee 1968-1970 (£'000)	0.699	0.630	1.3529*
Standard deviation	0.058	0.120	

* difference significantly different at 10% (one-tailed)
**significant at 5% (one-tailed)

The test used here was the parametric t test for studying differences between the means of two small samples. See Mason, R.D. (1978). Statistical Techniques in Business and Economics, 4th ed. R.D. Irwin, Homewood, Illinois. pp.294-6.

The differences in the mean values between the two groups were all in the expected direction with the exception of indicator ii. above relating to profits maintenance, although the difference here was not significant. This measure was used to try to determine if, regardless of the actual level of profits, diversification had allowed firms to maintain their existing level of profitability. On this basis the answer, perhaps surprisingly, appears to be no. With regard to the other indicators, iii. was significant at 10%, indicating that diversification, although apparently not significantly contributing to increased profitability, did reduce the time variability of profits.   Indicators v., vi. and vii. above present an interesting contrast, and also reinforce the need to use different measures of size in this area of statistical testing. The difference in the mean annual asset growth rates was significant at 5% in the expected direction. However, the sales growth rates were not significantly different, and neither were those for employment. The most plausible explanation for this is the more capital intensive nature of the activities of the diversified companies; and it would thus be rash to conclude that in any other sense diversification had contributed to growth. Thus the results relating to diversification and growth in respect of this sample of firms do not confirm the general impression gained in other studies.

It was also decided to test at this stage the hypothesis that diversification and size might be related. The assumption of a relationship between size and diversification seems fairly

plausible (Hassid, 1975). Large firms are likely to have the
professional staff expertise and access to new capital with
which to plan and finance diversification. The divorce
between control and ownership in such firms may not only
result in as great if not a greater emphasis upon growth than
in smaller firms, but also widen the area of perceived market
opportunities beyond the confines of a single industry, giving
such firms in Penrose terms an enlarged "productive opportunity"
(Penrose, 1980). The results for this group of firms on diversification and size are presented as indicator viii. in Table
3.7 above, and show quite clearly that there was no difference
in opening size between the diversified and non-diversified
companies. While in respect of each size measure diversified
firms were indeed larger than non-diversified (in terms of assets and sales they were twice as large), there was such a
diversity of size within each group that one cannot argue that
the two groups were significantly different in size.

Finally in Table 3.7 (indicator ix.) the average incomes per
employee in the opening part of the period 1968-1977 (1968-
1970) were compared between the two groups of firms. This was
done in order indirectly to test the hypothesis that a high
technical personnel ratio or quality of staff might be con-
ducive to a policy of diversification on the part of a firm.
That is, as in the case of firm size, the diversification
variable is dependent upon a high technical personnel ratio
as suggested by some authors (George, 1972). For our purpose
the independent variable is the average income per employee in
each firm over the period 1968-1970 expressed in 1967 terms by
reference to the index of earnings for employees in the jute
industry given in Appendix Table 4.3 of Chapter 4. The case
for adopting this variable is that higher incomes per employee
may indicate either that the workforce as a whole within the
firm is more highly paid than that of others, or that if shop-
floor wages are similar between firms then companies with
higher incomes per employee have a greater proportion of their
total workforce accounted for by more highly paid managerial
staff. In either case, but more particularly the latter, one
would assume that such a higher level of average incomes per
employee would be associated with a higher quality of staff
which may in various ways assist the firm in following a
policy of diversification. In fact the data on this variable
in Table 3.7 indicate that there was a significant difference
in the levels of incomes per employee between our two groups
of firms.

Multiple linear regression was also used to try to establish
the contribution of diversification to profitability, profit
variability (as measured in Table 3.7) and growth (of sales).

Three linear multiple regression equations were used.

     1. Profitability = f(Size, Growth, Diversification)
     2. Profit variability = f(Size, Growth, Diversification)
     3. Growth = f(Size, Profits, Diversification).

Using this analysis, and incorporating diversification as a
dummy variable having a value of 1 for Diversified firms and 0
for Non-diversified firms, yields the following results.

TABLE 3.8 Linear Regression of Profits, Growth, Size and
          Diversification

Dependent variable: Profitability

	Constant	b*	t	r*
Size (average)	7.8	0.00011	0.6958	0.2054
Growth	(1.2581)	0.91244	2.9965**	0.6704
Diversification		0.74073	0.2130	0.0641

    Multiple R^2 = 0.5164   F = 3.916**   DW = 2.2261

* partial coefficient   ** significant at 5%.

The Durbin-Watson statistic is used to test for serial correlation among the residuals in the least squares regression.
That is, it seeks to detect any curvilinear relationship
between the dependent variable and the independent variable(s)
when the regression equation is measuring the linear relationship. For all of the regression equations in this chapter a
two-tailed test for auto-correlation has been used, and unless
otherwise indicated the test reveals an absence of such auto-
correlation at the 10% level. See Merrill, W.C. and K.A. Fox
(1970). Introduction to Economic Statistics. Wiley, New
York. pp.415-6.

TABLE 3.9 Linear Regression of Profit Variability, Size,
          Growth and Diversification

Dependent variable : Profit Variability

	Constant	b*	t	r*
Size (average)	130.89	-0.00236	0.8149	-0.2384
Growth	(1.1934)	-6.05879	1.1318	-0.3230
Diversification		-56.04758	0.9170	-0.2665

    Multiple R^2 = 0.2897   F = 1.496   DW = 2.4951

* partial coefficient

TABLE 3.10   Linear Regression of Growth, Size, Profits and
                      Diversification

Dependent variable: Growth

	Constant	b*	t	r*
Size (opening)	-4.5	-0.00016	0.6928	-0.2045
Profitability	(0.9889)	0.50194	3.1157***	0.6847
Diversification		1.70579	0.6900	0.2037

Multiple R^2 = 0.5255   F = 4.061**   DW = 2.5715

* partial coefficient ** significant at 5%
*** significant at 1%.

With regard to the contribution of diversification in the
multiple regression in Tables 3.8 to 3.10, although again the
signs of the b coefficients are in the expected direction,
none of them is significant at 10%, and only in the case of
profit variability does the partial correlation coefficient
suggest that diversification offers any reasonable contribution to explaining differences in company performance.

TABLE 3.11   Zero Order and Partial Correlation Coefficients
                      with Diversification

	Profits	Profit Variability	Growth	Size (average)
Partial	0.2733	-0.3730	-0.1387	0.0028
Zero Order	0.2474	-0.2784	0.3093	0.4949

The data in Table 3.11 emphasise the need for the use of
partial correlation coefficients. These correlation coefficients, relating diversification to profits etc. do so
(in our case) on the statistical basis of the other variables
being equal to all firms. This is particularly necessary
when some of the other variables are related both to each
other and to diversification. For example, size is fairly
closely related to both profit variability and to diversification: the (zero order) Spearman rank correlation coefficients of average size (by sales) with profit variability and
diversification are -0.5321 and 0.4949 respectively. The
partial correlation coefficient table above gives one a
measure of the relationship between diversification alone
(and not size) and profit variability.

Finally, with regard to linear regression, diversification
was treated as the dependent variable, and profitability,
size, growth and employee incomes were chosen as independent
variables. The total degree of explanatoriness of these four
independent variables was low, and the DW statistic revealed

signs of autocorrelation. This latter finding is not of
course surprising given the dichotomous nature of the dependent variable. The detailed results were as follows.

TABLE 3.12   Linear Regression of Diversification Profitability,
Size, Growth and Employee Incomes

Dependent variable: Diversification

	Constant	b*	t	r*
Profitability	−0.51	0.00532	0.1983	0.0626
Opening Size (Sales)	(0.9273)	0.00000	0.1993	0.0629
Growth (Sales)		0.01683	0.4544	0.1422
Average Wage (1968-70)		1.43670	0.8024	0.2460

Multiple R^2 = 0.1979   F = 0.6166   DW = 0.8586

* partial coefficient.

These results indicate quite clearly that factors economic or
managerial other than those included in the present analysis
may have a much greater impact upon diversification than those
chosen above. Indeed interestingly if one analyses the data
for Table 3.12 in terms of stepwise regression, then of the
degree of explanatoriness of 19.79% (R^2) offered by the independent variables taken together, 13.70% out of 19.79% is
contributed by the fourth independent variable relating to
employee incomes. Also from Table 3.12 there appears,
perhaps surprisingly in the light of the circumstances of
this individual industry, to be no indication that firms
which wished to grow found it necessary to diversify.

Nonparametric tests are particularly suitable for investigat-
ing a phenomenon such as diversification where we are concerned with a variable which can be measured only on a
nominal or classificatory scale (in our case firms are either
Diversified or Non-diversified), and where the number of observations is small. We therefore tested for the impact of
diversification upon profitability, profit variability and
growth, using nonparametric tests relating to two independent
samples, and applying one-tailed tests of significance in the
directions indicated in the foregoing analysis using parametric tests.

The results of the nonparametric tests were as follows.

TABLE 3.13   Nonparametric Tests of Diversification

Association of Diversification with:	Fisher's Exact D	Mann-Whitney U*	Random-isation t**	Rho
Profitability	2	0.198	1.0455	0.2474
Growth (Sales)	3	0.232	1.1250	0.3093
Profit Variability	5	0.168	1.4405***	-0.2784
Opening Size (Sales)	2****	0.036****	0.7143	0.4021***
Average Wage 1968-70	2	0.095***	1.3529***	0.3712***

   *results given in terms of probability of observed U and
    under H_o, one-tailed test.
  **this t is to be interpreted on a nonparametric basis. On
    this and on these tests in general see Siegel, S. (1956).
    Nonparametric Tests for the Behavioural Sciences. McGraw-
    Hill Kogakusha, Tokyo, Ch. 6.
 ***significant at 10%, one-tailed.
****significant at 5%, one-tailed.

The results of these tests confirm many of our earlier statistical conclusions on the impact of diversification both as an
independent and as a dependent variable. There appears on
the basis of the nonparametric tests to be some evidence of
the relationship between diversification and profit variability in the expected direction, and, in contrast to the findings in Table 3.12 above, evidence of a relationship between
diversification and firm size, together with support for the
influence of the "personnel quality" variable.

       CONCLUSIONS

The bulk of the material in this chapter has been concerned
with reporting the results of an analysis of diversification
strategies at a number of levels. The final section affords
an opportunity to knit together a number of themes which has
emerged. Rather than summarising the findings of previous
sections, the purpose of the conclusions section is to draw
simultaneously upon those approaches to analysing diversification conduct. The themes which have emerged in this chapter are the need for diversification in a declining market,
the directions of diversification, the characteristics of
diversifying firms, the contribution of diversification to
company performance, and the problems encountered by firms in
pursuing diversification strategies.

No market which contracted so rapidly as that for traditional
jute products could do so without imposing the need for considerable adjustment on the companies involved. Company
deaths on a fairly significant scale followed the onset of

technological competition from polypropylene in the late 1960's. However, diversification has not been totally necessary for survival in the market. Some three or four companies (including one fairly large unit) have survived without the adoption of new technology. It must also be remembered that jute continues to be a fairly significant part of the operations of firms such as Don Bros. Buist, and Scott & Robertson, as well as Sidlaw and Craiks who have sought new markets for jute in the area of decorative wallcoverings. Thus despite diversifying firms continuing with jute operations, spinning and weaving of jute alone has for some businesses been a viable strategy for survival.

So far as directions of diversification are concerned, the product which displaced jute from many of its end-use areas - polypropylene - has not been adopted by all firms. For some businesses carpet manufacturing and engineering operations have taken the place of jute with success in the longer term.

Obviously, however, the major strategy followed by continuing firms in the market has been that of diversification into polypropylene - either weaving slit tape into cloth or also undertaking the extrusion of polypropylene film. One question which arises is whether those surviving firms which have diversified can be identified by any particular statistical characteristic. Firm size is one such variable which suggests itself; either in terms of the effect of the size variable itself or other company characteristics which may accompany size, such as a separation of professional management control from hereditary family ownership. Existing share of the traditional jute market may be another important variable regarding the extent of diversification. Family management, however, is such a pervasive characteristic of this industry that one cannot use its incidence as a means of distinguishing between diversifying and non-diversifying firms. In particular, some of the most successful diversifying firms of all sizes over the period from the mid 1960's to the mid 1970's were controlled and led by shareholding entrepreneurs. One thinks here of the Tough family at Scott & Fyfe, the Low family at Don Bros. Buist, and the Low and Bonar families in the Low & Bonar Group. Company size, as analysed in Tables 3.7 and 3.12, is not a significant determinant of diversification; although the results of the nonparametric tests contradict this. In some respects the finding of the parametric tests is surprising, as one might have thought that in respect of a diversification strategy requiring adoption of a new technology which was not only more definitely "science-based" than jute, but also significantly more capital intensive, size would have been a considerable advantage, or even

something of a prerequisite for successful diversification.
Utton (1977) in his study found some evidence of a positive
relationship between diversification and company size among
the top 200 U.K. manufacturing enterprises in 1974. The relationship appears to apply across all S.I.C. manufacturing
industry orders, but is not generally a very strong one. In
the case of our sample of firms casual observation does not
suggest a strong relationship in this direction, and parametric statistical analysis is made difficult by the smallness
of the sample and the skewed size distribution of the firms.
This may be a particular case where the findings of the nonparametric tests are more reliable. However, in our industry
despite the need for large capital sums for investment in
polypropylene weaving (around £32,000 per 5-metre loom in
1977), neither large initial capital requirements nor economies of scale (or diseconomies through operating at a relatively small scale or low degree of vertical integration) seem
to have constituted barriers to the entry of some smaller
firms to the league of diversifiers. So far as the influence
of existing market share of the traditional jute industry is
concerned and its impact upon diversification policy, those
firms which were dominant in the former market - such as Sidlaw, and Scott & Robertson - appear to have put more effort
into remaining in the market than other businesses, large or
small, whose dependence upon jute was less. While in one
sense this is not surprising, it does on the other hand
suggest that even where a firm is otherwise well equipped for
diversification, a high market share in the traditional industry may act as a brake upon necessary adjustment to new technologies and markets.

An obvious question in this analysis is, did diversification
help firms to grow, to increase profits or reduce profit
variability? None of the results of the tests gives conclusive positive evidence on this. Although the results in
Table 3.7 and the nonparametric tests in Table 3.13 suggest
that diversified firms did achieve lower profit variability,
no such result appeared from the regression analysis in
Table 3.9. Likewise Tables 3.8 and 3.10 revealed no relationship on a multivariate basis between diversification and
either profitability or growth (of sales) when other factors
such as size, growth and profitability were taken into
account. These results could be the outcome of misclassifi-
cation of the firms in Table 3.6. This, however, is not felt
likely to be a major factor. It may more likely be the case
that the results of diversification among firms following
this policy have taken some time to come through - much
longer than the 10-year period analysed; or that not diversifying may in the short run produce not dissimilar results

from diversifying, i.e. poor or variable profitability, or low growth (of sales). Furthermore, if the strategy of diversification was commenced by our Diversified population at different times within the 1968-1977 period, and if the results of such policies came on stream at different speeds, this would tend to produce a very heterogeneous performance by those diversified firms - for which hypothesis there is some evidence in Table 3.7.

A final theme which has persisted through the case studies has been that of the difficulties of managing some diversified interests, the encountering of unexpected problems, and the much-longer-than-expected time for the emergence of profits from new ventures. Engineering, interestingly, is an area into which many traditional jute firms have entered, but in which few have been successful in the long term. Don Bros. Buist, Halley, Thomson Shepherd, and H. & A. Scott are examples of companies which have either entered and left the engineering industry within the last 15 years, or whose engineering subsidiaries appear to have remained relatively unsuccessful.

In general, management of diversifying firms appear to have encountered a number of unforeseen technical problems in diversifying; and a further common experience among such firms has been the failure of diversified areas of business to generate earnings sufficiently quickly to compensate either for the large amounts of invested capital or to cover declining profits in traditional textiles. The prospect of this hiatus may have discouraged or precluded smaller firms from following a policy of diversification. Although this situation has been commented on in the case studies by the chairmen of nearly all of the major firms, the data which perhaps best illustrate the problem are those of a smaller company.

TABLE 3.14   William Halley & Sons Ltd.

	Spinning, Manufacturing and Merchanting of Textiles*		Distribution of Motor Cars, Agricultural and Horticultural Implements	
	Sales (£'000)	Margin** (%)	Sales (£'000)	Margin** (%)
1968	2,420	6.4	1,632	1.2
1969	2,159	6.2	1,708	1.0
1970	1,946	2.2	1,955	1.8
1971	2,536	(3.0)	2,017	1.6
1972	3,707	1.6	2,816	2.3
1973	4,601	1.8	3,379	2.8
1974	5,294	6.0	3,359	2.8
1975	4,181	0.6	5,405	2.9
1976	4,994	6.5	6,750	2.5
1977	5,773	7.1	9,021	4.4

 * In the case of Halley this includes synthetics as well as
   jute.
** Profit Margin is the pre-tax profit in each sales area as
   a proportion of turnover.

Source: Company Annual Reports & Accounts.

In the absence of data for capital employed in each area, one
can only note the gradual buildup of non-textile sales: from
some 40% in 1968 to around half in 1971, and to about 61% in
1977.   In respect of average profit margins, the 10-year
arithmetic mean for Textiles was 3.5% compared with 2.3% for
non-textile activities;   although the variability is greater
with respect to Textiles, and there is a more distinctly upward trend in the non-textile area.   The chairman of the
company himself in this case emphasised the long-term nature
of the rewards from diversification, and the short-term
pressures on profits and liquidity.   Such problems were due
(William Halley & Sons, 1972 Annual Report) "in the main to
the time lag between building up profitable diversifications,
which utilise much capital, whilst at the same time maintaining the capital employed in our jute manufacturing activity,
which is declining in profitability".

As a final point, it may be noted that, although this study
has not been able to shed any light on some of the more
sophisticated hypotheses regarding diversification, such as
the relative contributions of internal and external expansion;
so far as the lack of a strong statistical relationship between
firm size, profits or profit variability and diversification,
or the tendency for an inverse relationship to exist between

industry growth and the extent of firm diversification, the
findings of this study are largely consistent with those of
more specialist analyses in the field.

The material in this chapter, dealing with the market conduct
or behaviour of firms, has allowed us to indulge in few generalisations. Admittedly there have been some common
features relating to the firms in the industry over the period
from the mid 1960's to 1977. Most, but by no means all, of
the surviving firms from the traditional jute industry have
entered the polypropylene field. For most of the diversifying
businesses, but again not for all, diversification has been a
difficult policy to implement, and for a variety of reasons
which this study has not been able fully to investigate.
Beyond this few generalisations are possible. Variables such
as the size of the firm, the quality of its workforce (and
perhaps especially of its management), or the attachment of a
business to the traditional jute industry may also have had
an influence on market conduct at the company level. We can
only conclude here that with respect to their response to the
rapid contraction of the jute industry local firms behaved in
a variety of ways with varied outcomes. The following chapter
seeks to examine these outcomes at the industry level in more
detail under the heading of market performance.

References

Dundee Chamber of Commerce Journal. Chamber of Commerce,
Dundee.

George, K.D. (1972). The changing structure of competitive
industry. Econ. Jour., 82, 355-7.

Gorecki, P.K. (1975). An inter-industry analysis of diversification. Jour. Ind. Econ., 24, 131-46.

Hassid, J. (1975). Recent evidence on conglomerate diversification in U.K. manufacturing industry. Manch.School, 43,
384-7.

Hassid, J. (1977). Diversification and the firm's rate of
growth. Manch. School, 45, 16-28.

Leveson, J.H. (1973). Industrial Organisation of the Jute
Manufacturing Industry: Decline and Diversification. College
of Technology, Dundee. pp. 7 and 16-17.

Manson, J. (1976). The Major Changes Undertaken by Caird
(Dundee) Ltd. in their Diversification. Unpublished D.M.S.
Dissertation, Dundee College of Technology. p.11.

Penrose, E.T. (1980). The Theory of the Growth of the Firm,
rev. ed. Blackwell, Oxford. p.31.

Utton, M.A. (1977). Large firm diversification in British
manufacturing industry. Econ. Jour., 87, 103-7.

CHAPTER 4

ECONOMIC PERFORMANCE

INTRODUCTION

The major concern of any economic study of an industry must
be the way in which the market has operated over a given
period. In more formal terms one is examining the resource-
allocation and welfare aspects of the market mechanism in a
particular area. The concern of the industrial organisation
economist is both less formally stated and more open-ended.
Bain for example (1968) defines market performance as "the
composite of end results which firms in any market arrive at
by pursuing whatever lines of conduct (or behaviour) they
espouse". Thus one purpose of presenting the material in
this chapter is to bring together data on such "end results"
which can be used in arriving at more general conclusions in
the final chapter. In this particular case the market performance has been analysed in terms of dimensions reflecting
company "financial" performance, the use of labour, investment and modernisation, and research and development. In the
final section in this chapter conclusions are offered on the
findings detailed in the earlier sections.

As usual in economics studies a severe limiting factor in the
analysis is the availability of raw data. None of these
below is perfect for the purpose for which it is used; but
the data are believed to be the best available. This situation with regard to raw data often means that the economic
conclusions cannot be as strongly drawn as one would like.
As the advice of R.G.D. Allen below indicates (1951), the
whole issue is one of judgement and balance: perhaps nowhere
more so than in the area of economics.

"The job of the statistician is to get material
of the greatest possible accuracy and then to
make the best use of it. He should not, however,
discard imperfect data if nothing better is
available. Not even the most subtle and skilful
analysis can overcome completely the unreliability
of basic data, but the best can always be made of
a bad job. Some material, so rough as to be insufficient for fine analysis, may still support
particular conclusions. The skilled statistician
knows where he can proceed and where he must
stop."

The analysis of market performance in this chapter is carried
out at a number of levels. The first function of the data is
simply to present measures of economic performance, the
characteristics or variables being chosen on the basis of
what microeconomic theory regards as being the relevant and
salient factors in exploring market performance. The variables chosen here are "financial" measures of performance,
measures of labour usage, measures of investment, and of
research and development. The data under these headings have
been drawn from both primary and secondary sources.

The second purpose of measuring market performance is to use
the data gathered as a basis for testing hypotheses based
upon microeconomic theory, and for establishing statistical
relationships. Thus in addition to simply measuring company
profitability, growth, labour productivity, and levels of
investment or research it is desirable to measure the trend
of the variables against time, to measure the degree of
association or explanatoriness between variables, and so to
arrive at conclusions regarding the relative importance of
the range of variables.

The third purpose of measuring individual aspects of market
performance in this study is to formulate conclusions both
with regard to performance overall and also in the context
of the study as a whole.

Although the individual statistical tests used in each case
will be discussed in their specific context, a word needs to
be said here about statistical tests in general. The type
of statistical tests required in this area of inquiry are
those which will measure trends, differences and association
so as to allow one to infer economic relationships from the
data. There are broadly speaking two types of tests
available: parametric and nonparametric. The former require

that certain assumptions be made about the population from
which the sample statistics are drawn. The most significant
for our purpose is that the data in the populations are normally distributed; the other principal one is that populations being compared have equal variances. There is evidence
to suggest that the former of these two conditions does not
hold for many economic data of the type being analysed here
(Whittington, 1971, pp.20-30; O'Brien and others,1979). Thus
for our purposes nonparametric or "distribution free" statistical tests are appropriate, and have been used along with the
more traditional parametric tests. It is also the case that
nonparametric tests are more appropriate where the number of
observations is fairly small, as is certainly the case in
this study (Siegel, 1958, pp.30-34).

COMPANY FINANCIAL PERFORMANCE

The function of this first section is to appraise the financial economic performance of those firms falling into the jute
industry category: performance here being defined by
reference to standard accounting ratios, and thus reflecting
only these aspects of a firm's performance.

One of the major difficulties here is that of linking company
financial performance as analysed below, and economic
efficiency, at either the firm, market or national level.
In some respects our additional analysis under other market
performance headings will enable us to qualify and extend
the results of the accounting analysis. One must nonetheless
bear in mind certain qualifications in assuming any correspondence between company and economy performance. These two
phenomena have been separated under the respective titles of
"business efficiency" and "economic efficiency" by Amey
(1969); and only under very restricted conditions, it is
argued, can the latter be equated with the former. In most
microeconomics studies a firm's profits (expressed as a
ratio of its capital employed) are accepted as a measure of
the efficiency or surplus created by the excess value of output over the value of the resources used. However, this
acceptance, when translated into market terms, ignores such
issues as whether the firm is operating at the most efficient
scale or point on its cost curve (technical efficiency), or
whether the best technical methods or market opportunities
available are being used or sought out (X-efficiency). It
also fails to recognise the value to society of the resources
which the firm has consumed (their opportunity cost); and
also the fact that the product or production process
employed by the firm (or the act of consumption by users of

the product) may have wider spillover effects, in the form of
costs or benefits, on the rest of society (the problem of
externalities). Finally, such acceptance also assumes that
firms are operating in structurally competitive markets -
where conditions of perfect or near perfect competition
obtain. Further "upsetting" conditions to this equating of
business and economic efficiency include the existence of
taxes or subsidies, import or export restrictions etc.
Nonetheless, the approach used here is to analyse company
accounting data over as great a proportion of the major
period of the study as possible in order to study business
efficiency as a proxy for economic efficiency.

It is also recognised, of course, that company accounting data
themselves are in many respects imperfect for purposes of
economic analysis. For example, not only is there little
correspondence between the economist's and the accountant's
concepts of business income and asset valuation; but within
the standard conventions of accounting practice there may be
a serious lack of comparability of data over time or between
the data relating to small firms and large businesses. It is
considered, however, that an examination of such data is indispensable in arriving at a view on company performance.
Furthermore, as one author (Meeks, 1977) has commented, and
whose work is largely based upon the use of company accounting
data, these figures are the results of considerable labour by
internal company accounting staff, are verified by the
auditing profession which itself ensures a degree of standard-
isation of company final accounts across the economy (or at
least within a single industry), and are anyhow the accepted
basis of much national income accounting data. Thus despite
the widely recognised pitfalls involved in using company
accounting data for economic analysis, it is felt that such
analysis is indispensable as a basis for broader conclusions
on the performance of this particular market.

The analysis of industry performance in terms of company
accounting data is perforce largely limited to the period 1968-
1977, since it was only with the coming into force of the 1967
Companies Act that company accounting data became statutorily
available in respect of smaller (private) companies; and it
is also only since that time that turnover and employment data
have had to be revealed by firms in their annual reports.
Data on profits, assets and sales (turnover) as well as on
employment have been used. These were obtained in respect of
16 firms which continued in existence from 1967 to 1977; and
data were abstracted directly by the author from the annual
returns made by the companies concerned and filed at Companies
House in London (prior to their remove to Cardiff) and

Edinburgh.   It has thus been possible to adopt with accuracy
the desired definitions of the data outlined above, and these
definitions are discussed in more detail below.

Profitability:

Although there is a number of flaws in its computation, the
most widely accepted measure of aggregate company performance
remains the rate of return on capital employed. In this study
the ratio was defined as the profits in any one year after
deduction of the usual business expenses (including directors'
fees and depreciation) but before deduction of interest on
preference shares, debentures, or long-term loans (including
bank borrowing), expressed as a ratio of the net assets of
the firm, defined correspondingly as total assets less non-
bank current liabilities. The ratio adopted here is a measure
of the return on the total invested capital in the business
without regard to the individual sources of finance. This is
felt to be the definition appropriate to the purpose of the
study.

Turning to the data on profits (i.e. the profitability ratios)
for the 16 firms over the period 1968-1977, three separate
areas of investigation suggest themselves. The first basic
question asked is, was there a trend of the profit ratios
over time? Second, was there any change in the profit
performance between the two sub-periods 1968-1972 and 1973-
1977? Third, what are the major explanatory variables (both
on a univariate and on a multivariate basis) with regard to
the profit performance of the 16 firms over the ten-year
period?

The initial attempt to answer the first question, on the
trend of profits, involved an analysis of the linear regression
of the unadjusted profit ratios of each of the 16 firms,
and also of the 16-firm average, against time. In this case
the significance and explanatory power of the linear
equations were so low that no conclusion as to the trend can
be drawn. Thus, using the standard parametric test for trend
(the b coefficient of this regression of profitability and
time) one cannot establish any discernible trend of the unadjusted profit ratios over this period.   So far as nonparametric tests are concerned, the Spearman test for rank
correlation indicated a significant relationship in the case
of only two firms out of 16.

The above analysis was carried out very much as a "trial run"
in order to determine whether any meaningful results arose
using unadjusted profits data. More interest centres around

the behaviour of "real" profit rates, i.e. adjusted for
changes in the general level of profits in the economy. The
conversion of the unadjusted to "real" profit rates was carried
out by constructing a time series of profit ratios for "Manufacturing Industries" from Business Monitor MA3 "Company
Finance". This time series, covering listed and unlisted
companies, was converted into index form (1967 = 100), and the
unadjusted profit ratios for each firm were multiplied by the
reciprocal of the above index for the appropriate year. The
result of this computation is a set of profit ratios for each
of the 16 firms which tells us how the firm was performing
"relative to manufacturing industry as a whole". To look at
it another way, changes in the general macro business environment have been eliminated. It may also be claimed that the
general tendency for inflation to increase "historic cost"
rates of return on capital employed has also been allowed for.
This type of correction, therefore, although not without
statistical flaws, is highly desirable in measuring profit
ratios over time, and is indeed absolutely essential if
comparisons of individual sub-period profit performance are
to be carried out (see below). The results of regressing such
data against time are little different from those using unadjusted data.   In all but two cases the slope of the regression was not significant at 10%. The Spearman coefficient
of rank correlation likewise failed to suggest any relationship with time.

The final, and admittedly rather crude, approach in measuring
the trend of profits was to use the sign of the b coefficient
in the linear regression equation for each of the 16 firms as
a means of measuring whether across the board there were, say,
more increases than decreases in profit rates over time.
On this basis nonparametric tests were adopted to indicate
whether for the 16 firms as a whole over the ten-year period
there was a generally upward or downward trend in profitability. The raw data were as follows.

TABLE 4.1 Sign of b Coefficient in Regression Equations

		Positive	Negative	Total
Profits Data:	Unadjusted	7	9	16
	Adjusted	6	10	16

The one-sample tests used were the binomial test and chi-
squared. These are nonparametric tests designed to measure
the extent to which an occurrence deviates from the expected:
in our case the null hypothesis being that there was no
trend - that one would expect from our group of 16 firms 8

increases and 8 decreases in the trend of profit rates over
the period.

TABLE 4.2   Probability of Observed Results Under Null
            Hypothesis

	Binomial Test	Chi Squared
Unadjusted	0.454	0.3
Real	0.804	0.5

These results confirm that neither on a parametric nor on a
nonparametric basis is there any indication of an upward or
downward trend in profits for those 16 surviving firms in the
jute industry over the decade to 1977.

The conclusions regarding economic performance which one can
draw from this analysis of profit trends must be tentative.
Nonetheless, even allowing for the ommission from our analysis
of those firms which "died" within the period, we can conclude
that those 16 continuing firms, which at the beginning of the
period accounted for about 85% of Dundee jute spinning and
weaving activity, did not as a group suffer any reduction in
profitability during a time when output of their traditional
product fell by around 65%. As was noted in Chapter 3 a major
response to the decline of the traditional jute market was
diversification. This strategy, although it was not pursued
by all firms, was adopted by the majority, and may thus have
contributed to the maintenance of profit levels over this
period.

Finally on this first aspect of profitability, the data on
adjusted profit ratios were used to calculate the intragroup
variability of profits. A simple time series of the variability of profits among the 16 firms in each of the ten years was
calculated and measured against time. This measure tells us
whether over the period the group of firms was becoming more
or less homogeneous with regard to profitability.

TABLE 4.3   Linear Regression of Intragroup Profit Variability
            and Time

Dependent Variable	b	t	R^2	Rho	DW*
Standard deviation	-0.1242	0.3493	0.0150	-0.1273	1.3793
Coeff.of variation	-1.5832	0.2374	0.0070	-0.0303	1.1937

*the Durbin-Watson statistic designed to test for serial cor-
relation among the residuals in O.L.S. regression. See
Merrill, W.C. and K.A. Fox (1970). Introduction to Economic

Statistics. Wiley, New York. pp.415-16. For all data in this
study serial correlation was tested for using a two-tailed
test. In this particular case the statistic was not significant at 10%, but was within the indeterminate range.

Table 4.3 above shows that the slope of the linear regression
equation in respect of both the standard deviation and the
coefficient of variation was negative but not significant.
The figures for R^2 are very low, and the Spearman coefficients
of rank correlation are negative but not significant. The
conclusion is that the variability of profits among the group
of firms did not change significantly over the period, telling
us that as a group of firms became neither more nor less
homogeneous with respect to profitability over the period
1968-1977.

Turning to the second major question under the heading of
profit performance, that of the performance of the firms over
the two subperiods 1968-1972 and 1973-1977, the first question
being asked is: assuming that we can break down the total 10-
year period into a first subperiod of initial adjustment to
the demise of the market for jute and the rise of polypropylene, and a second subperiod of consolidation of diversification strategies where appropriate, is it possible to identify
these periods by reference to the profit performance of the
firms? Comparison was made of the means of the real or
adjusted profit ratios in each of the two subperiods for each
firm and also in respect of the 16-firm average. It should be
noted that in respect of all measures of mean profit rates it
is the arithmetic rather than the geometric mean which is used.
This is necessary because of the incidence of negative rate of
return, i.e. losses, in a number of instances. Using the
normal (two-tailed) t test, in no single case among the 16
firms were the subperiod average profit ratios significantly
different at 5% (no more were significant at 10%). Additionally the two subperiod means of the 16 firms were treated as
16 paired observations. The appropriate t test applied to
these data likewise failed to yield significant results (t =
1.2353 where df = 15) (Daniel and Terrell, 1975).

TABLE 4.4   Probability of Observed Results Under Null
            Hypothesis

                Sign Test   0.804
                Wilcoxon   T = 51.5

Table 4.4 gives the results of the nonparametric tests applied
to the subperiod profitability data. Neither the Sign Test
nor the Wilcoxon Matched-Pairs Signed-Ranks Test suggest that

the null hypothesis that there was no difference between the
adjusted profit ratio means for the two subperiods can be
disproved. It must therefore generally be concluded that for
the continuing firms in the industry over this period there
was no significant change in the mean profit levels from one
subperiod to another.

A second, closely related issue under this general heading of
subperiod profit analysis is that of the maintenance by firms
of their profit levels relative to one another, and also that
of whether profitability in the latter subperiod is in any
sense the outcome of profitability in the former. The first
issue was examined by means of the Spearman coefficient of
rank correlation. Rho was calculated in respect of the 16
pairs of subperiod rates of return. The value of the coefficient was 0.5559, which on a two-tailed basis is significant at 5%. This suggests that there was considerable relative stability of profit levels within the group over the two
5-year subperiods.

Looking at the question of the linear relationship between
profits in the latter subperiod (as the dependent variable)
and profits in the former, one is not necessarily suggesting
a causal relationship between the two. This could only be
hypothesised if, for example, profits in the earlier subperiod created growth which transferred a firm into a higher
size class, which in turn was associated with increased
profitability. What any linear association may, however,
suggest is a persistency in a later period of the factors
which determined the level of profits in an earlier one.
The linear regression in respect of the two subperiods for
our group of firms was as follows.

TABLE 4.5 Linear Regression of Average Profit Ratios in Two
           Subperiods

Constant	b	t	R^2	DW
6.0	0.5361	3.7359*	0.4991	2.0193**

* significant at 1%; ** not significant at 10%.

Table 4.5 indicates a significant positive relationship
between profits in the two subperiods, with around 50% of
the variation in average profitability in 1973-1977 being
explained by relative profitability 1968-1972. The b coefficient of less than unity suggests a degree of regression
in profitability over the two periods. Companies which performed well 1968-1972 also performed well 1973-1977 but not

to the same extent, and similarly for poor performers.

These two pieces of analysis again suggest that there was
little disturbance in the profit position of the firms over
the two subperiods; and therefore reinforce our earlier conclusion that in terms of relative (i.e. adjusted) profitability the period 1968-1977 was not a particularly upsetting one
for the industry.

The third question to be answered in the context of the
analysis of profitability is, what appear to have been the
major determinants of profitability and profit variability in
the industry? Using data in respect of the 15 firms for which
all the necessary information was available, and taking firstly
the 10-year average level of profitability (1968-1977) as the
dependent variable, size (in terms of opening and average
assets and sales) and growth (also in terms of both assets and
sales) were used as possible independent variables.

In the case of the size variables, on no occasion was the t
statistic relating to the b coefficient significant at 10%,
and the values of R^2 (the coefficient of determination) were
low. The effect of growth on average profits over the period
was much more pronounced. The t statistic in respect of the
b coefficient was significant at 1% with regard to both asset
and sales growth, and the coefficient of determination in each
case was around 50%. A similar distinction in impact was
brought out using multiple linear regression and including
size and growth simultaneously as independent variables.
This multivariate analysis is essential if one is to distinguish clearly the separate impact of more than one independent variable where there may be a relationship among
the independent variables themselves.

TABLE 4.6 Multiple Regression of Profitability, Size and Growth

Dependent variable: 10-year average profit ratio

Independent Variables	Constant	b*	t	r*
Size (average assets)	4.3	0.00011	0.5186	0.1481
Growth (assets)		0.55533	3.2724***	0.6866
		Multiple R^2 = 0.4957 F = 5.897**		
		DW = 2.2465****		
Size (average)	-0.7	0.00009	0.7959	0.2239
Growth (sales)		0.93690	3.7193***	0.7318
		Multiple R^2 = 0.5603 F = 7.646***		
		DW = 2.0903****		

* partial coefficients;   ** significant at 5%;
*** significant at 1%;   **** not significant at 10%.

For this particular group of firms over this period we can conclude that size was not a significant determinant of profitability, but that there was a significant positive linear
relationship between growth and profits.

The general findings in this area of the impact of size and
growth on profitability so far as U.K. data are concerned are
still a matter of some dispute. We may conclude, however,
that our findings on the profits-size relationship are not in
conflict with those of most U.K. studies (Howe, 1978, pp.86-
87).

With regard to profit variability over the period, this was
measured in terms of the simple time variability of profits
(the standard deviation about the 10-year mean), the time
variability relative to the mean (the coefficient of variation),
and also the variability around the linear trend of profits as
measured by the residual variance about the trend.

TABLE 4.7   Linear Regression of Profit Variability and Size

Dependent Variable: standard deviation of 10-year profit ratios)

Independent Variable	Constant	b	t	R^2	DW**
Average assets	8.9	-0.00028	1.5984	0.1642	1.6795
Opening assets	8.9	-0.00052	1.5409	0.1545	1.6711
Average sales	9.0	-0.00015	1.6498	0.1731	1.7026
Opening sales	9.0	-0.00027	1.5864	1.1622	1.7076

Dependent variable: coeff. of variation of 10-year profit ratios

Average assets	86.2	-0.00293	1.8363*	0.2059	1.8986
Opening assets	85.9	-0.00529	1.6935	0.1807	1.9333
Average sales	88.0	-0.00162	1.9742*	0.2307	1.8928
Opening sales	87.7	-0.00288	1.7504	0.1984	1.8904

Dependent variable: residual variance about 10-year linear
                    trend

Average assets	101.9	-0.00457	1.1505	0.0924	2.0867
Opening assets	102.3	-0.00863	1.1227	0.0884	2.0758
Average sales	104.7	-0.00251	1.2137	0.1018	2.0426
Opening sales	104.7	-0.00459	1.1837	0.0973	2.0185

* significant at 10%;   ** not significant at 10%.

These results show that, using parametric tests, size had the
effect of reducing profit variability at any level of significance only if this was measured in terms of the coefficient

of variation with size measured in terms of average values.
As in the case of the profits-size analysis, this finding is
not out of line with those of U.K. studies generally (Howe,
1978, pp.86-87).

Finally in this analysis of profitability, the relationship
between profits and size or growth, and profit variability
and size was checked using a number of nonparametric tests.
Of such tests available for testing hypotheses about two
independent samples, four were chosen which were appropriate
for testing differences in central tendency among populations
of our size. These are the Fisher Exact Probability Test,
the Mann-Whitney U Test, the Randomisation Test and Spearman's Rho (Siegel, 1968, Ch.6). These nonparametric tests
were used to duplicate the analysis of the impact of size
upon profitability and profit variability, the fuller analysis
of the profits-growth relationship being delayed until the
next subsection on growth. The results of the nonparametric
tests are presented in Table 4.8.

We are now in a position to summarise the findings on profit
performance for this group of firms over the period 1968-1977.
These findings may be stated briefly as follows.

1.   There was no significant upward or downward
      trend of profits over the period relative to
      U.K. manufacturing industry as a whole.

2.   As measured by both the standard deviation
      and coefficient of variation of the intra-
      group profit ratios in each year, there was
      no trend of increased or decreased homo-
      geneity of the group as regards firm profit-
      ability over the period.

3.   Considering the two subperiods 1968-1972 and
      1973-1977, there were no significant differ-
      ences in profit performance among the firms
      over the two subperiods.

4.   The relative profitability of the firms to
      one another within the group, as measured by
      the Spearman rank correlation coefficient, did
      not change significantly over the two sub-
      periods.

5.   There was a significant linear relationship
      between the 16-firm set of average profit
      ratios for the two subperiods.

6.   This particular group of firms over the period
     1968-1977 displayed no significant relation-
     ship between size and profitability, or between
     size and profit variability, although the non-
     parametric tests whose results are summarised
     in Table 8 did suggest that there was a
     relationship between firm size and profit
     variability over time. It was also noted that
     there was a significant positive linear
     relationship between growth and profits,
     supported by the results of the nonparametric
     tests.

TABLE 4.8   Nonparametric Analysis of Profits, Profit Varia-
            bility and Size

	Fisher's Exact D	Mann-Whitney U	Random-isation t	Rho
Profitability and Size:				
Average assets	1	16	1.2272	0.2821
Opening assets	2	11	1.2400	0.0036
Average sales	1	13	1.3333	0.2929
Opening sales	3	20	0.8085	0.1500
Profitability and Growth:				
Assets	1*	11**	2.0750*	0.6130**
Sales	1*	13**	1.9000*	0.6857***
Profit Variability and Size:				
i. Standard deviation:				
Average assets	O	7**	2.0000*	-0.6988***
Opening assets	O	10	1.3793	-0.5179**
Average sales	1**	10*	1.5484	-0.5702**
Opening sales	O**	10**	2.7917**	-0.5845**
ii. Coefficient of variation:				
Average assets	O*	2***	3.1535***	-0.7143***
Opening assets	1	12	0.7946	-0.4500*
Average sales	2	10**	1.6163	-0.6393***
Opening sales	3	18	1.0854	-0.5000*
iii. Residual variance:				
Average assets	O	8**	1.5787	-0.6679***
Opening assets	O	15	1.1960	-0.5643**
Average sales	O*	12*	2.0635*	-0.5321**
Opening sales	O*	14	2.2478**	-0.5643**

Significance levels: *10%,   **5%,   *** 1%.

The general picture which emerges then is one of stability of

profit performance so far as this group of firms is concerned.
The profits and profit variability-size relationship is also
consistent with comparable U.K. studies. Even accepting that
we are studying the performance of a surviving continuing
group of firms (data on those firms which died during the
period are not available), some of the results are still a
little surprising.

Growth:

The growth variable must be regarded as a particularly important measure of company performance in an industry where the
traditional market has been characterised by rapid decline.
Growth on the part of an individual firm under such conditions implies either superior performance within the traditional market (significantly increasing market share), or
successful diversification in moving into new market areas.

Singh and Whittington in their econometric study of firm
growth (1968) distinguish between willingness and ability to
grow on the part of firms. The former characteristic,
willingness, reminds one that not all management/ownership
classes of business may have a high desire or incentive to
grow; and since the pattern of ownership or management is
likely to be related to firm size, with smaller businesses
being owner-managed, this suggests that on this ground at
least growth may be a function of firm size. With regard to
profitability and growth, one would expect a fairly close
causal relationship from the former to the latter. On the
basis of a very simple financial model involving no access
to new outside funds (which may not depart so far from
reality for our population of firms) the maximum asset growth
rate, g, is determined by the product of the profitability
of capital employed and the extent of corporate savings.
Thus, $g = (P/K)(R/P)$ where P = profits, K = capital employed,
and R = retentions. It would be accepted that the thinking
behind this expression can be extended to include cases
where growth can also be financed externally, as shareholders (existing and potential), debenture holders and
bankers will all regard past profit performance by a business
as a primary indicator in arriving at their lending decision.

There are two aspects of growth to be examined here. First,
what appear to be the causal factors behind growth for our
group of firms, and in particular what are the roles of size
and profitability? Second, is there any evidence of persistency of growth within the total period 1968-1977? Looking
at the first question, data on assets and sales, and on

growth of assets and sales were used for the 15 firms for
whom these were available. Sales data were expressed in 1967
terms by reference to the Index of Wholesale Prices (Textiles),
and assets were also expressed in 1967 terms by reference to
Price Index Numbers for Current Cost Accounting (Textiles,
Leather & Clothing). This enabled one to distinguish between
the volume growth of assets and sales. It may be argued that
the relationship between profitability and growth measured by
employment contains a number of complexities concerning labour
productivity and profitability. Nonetheless employment data
were included for comparative purposes.

The use of both asset and sales data as growth measures was
thought necessary as a cross check for a number of reasons.
First, expansion of assets by a firm may indicate a movement
from labour- to capital-intensive methods of production
rather than expansion of the scale of an enterprise. Second,
a company which is profitable, and which does not pay out all
profits as dividend, is by definition expanding its assets
base by adding to retained earnings, thus creating a spurious
and tautological relationship between profitability and asset
growth. This would be particularly so if, as in our case,
assets are measured at year-end values. Third, it has been
pointed out that different measures of firm size are only
"interchangeable" (i.e. the findings in the type of analysis
below are independent of the actual measure of firm size
used) if the measures are proportional to each other. This
assumes that for two input measures of firm size, for example
assets and employment, the production function is homothetic -
i.e. the isoquants lie parallel to one another and thus the
expansion path is linear. Homotheticity is not something
which one can assume a priori. Indeed there would appear to
be evidence to the contrary (Smyth, Boyes and Peseau, 1975,
Chs. 1 and 2). Likewise, the proportionality of measures of
firm size such as assets (input) and sales (output) is likely
to be upset by the presence of economies of scale, for the
existence of which there is considerable evidence (Pratten,
1971). A final problem in using assets as a measure of firm
growth in the context of size-growth-profitability studies
is that there is some evidence that larger firms revalue their
assets more frequently than smaller firms. Such revaluations
obviously overstate the growth performance and understate the
profitability ratio of larger businesses (Whittington, 1971,
pp.59-65). Fortunately the general conclusion in Whittington's
study was that this tendency did not seriously bias the
results. In the case of our population the asset revaluations
which had occurred had indeed been carried out by the largest
firms. These were, however, minimal and were not corrected
for in the asset data used in the tests.

The first part of the regression analysis involved adopting size as the single explanatory variable in respect of growth. The results are presented in Table 4.9 below.

TABLE 4.9 Linear Regression of Growth and Opening Size

Dependent variable: 10-year average annual real growth rate
                    1968-1977*

Size (opening)	Constant	b	t	R^2	DW**
Assets	-2.5	0.00018	0.2899	0.0064	1.7944
Sales	0.01	0.00005	0.2175	0.0036	1.9888
Employment	-2.0	-0.00026	0.2226	0.0038	2.4977

* in the case of employment the period is 1969-1977 as no
  1967 data were available; ** not significant at 10%.

Size appears to explain no significant amount of growth, either in terms of assets, sales or employment. This leads one to the interesting conclusion that, in this market where growth predominantly implied adoption of new technology and significant new investment, firms which were initially large performed no better over the period than their smaller competitors.

The data imply that the performance of firms in this group over the period complied with Gibrat's Law: that the proportionate rate of growth of the firm is independent of initial size. It was decided to test for this explicitly (Smith, Boyes and Peseau, 1975, Ch. 4). The test here is to regress the opening and closing size values in terms of their natural logarithms. In our case the equation is

$$x_i(1977) = a + bx_i(1968)$$

where x_i represents the various measures of firm size expressed in the form of natural logarithms. If b equals 1, or is not significantly different from 1, then firm growth rate is independent of opening size. The results are reported below.

TABLE 4.10 Linear Regression of Natural Logarithms of
            Opening and Closing Firm Size

Size Measure	Constant	b	t*
Assets	-0.178	0.9862	0.0746
Sales	-0.040	1.0129	0.1076
Employment	0.253	0.9248	0.5905

* with respect to 1

Since in no case is the t statistic in Table 4.10 significant
we may conclude that b is not significantly different from
unity, and thus that the performance of our group of firms
complied with Gibrat's Law. This result is not in conflict
with general findings regarding the relationship between firm
size and growth. Over different time periods and using different samples of companies slightly different conclusions
have been reached by different authors. A fair summary of
these studies, however, would be that no clear relationship
has emerged between firm size and growth rates (Howe, 1978,
pp.87-8).

We now turn to profitability as an explanatory variable in
respect of growth.

TABLE 4.11   Linear Regression of Growth and Profitability

Dependent variable: growth

Growth Measure	Constant	b	t	R^2	DW***
Assets	-9.8	0.8092	3.8406**	0.5316	2.4647
Sales	-5.1	0.5547	3.5808**	0.4966	2.5989
Employment	-6.5	0.4528	2.8954*	0.3920	2.9699

* significant at 5%; ** significant at 1%; not significant
  at 10%; in the case of Employment the DW statistic is
  within the indeterminate range.

Table 4.11 emphasises by contrast with Tables 4.9 and 4.10 the
very significant role of profitability in explaining differences in average growth rates among our group of firms over
the period 1968-1977 when relative growth may be taken as a
very significant aspect of market performance by individual
firms.

Although we have found no significant relationship between
profits and size for this group of firms, it was decided to
conduct a multiple regression analysis of growth, profitability and size in order clearly to identify the separate impact
of profitability and size upon growth. The results of this
analysis are reported in Table 4.12.

TABLE 4.12 Multiple Regression Analysis of Growth, Size and
            Profitability

Independent Variables	Constant	b*	t	r*	DW ****
Size (Assets)	-9.6	-0.00015	0.3317	-0.0953	2.5770
Profitability		0.82380	3.6991***	0.7330	
Size (Sales)	-4.8	-0.00008	0.4938	-0.1411	2.8650≠
Profitability		0.57278	3.4968***	0.7105	
Size (Employment)	-6.0	-0.00068	0.7361	-0.2079	3.1470
Profitability		0.47149	2.9249**	0.6450	

* partial coefficients; ** significant at 5%; *** significant
  at 1%; **** not significant at 10%; ≠ within indeterminate
  range.

Table 4.12 highlights the impact of profits as an explanatory
variable in respect of growth when the impact of size has been
"held constant".   It should be noted that the t value in
respect of the size variable itself when considered along with
profitability is much greater in the case of labour than assets
or sales. However, the relative effect of the profitability
variable is in the opposite direction. The coefficients of
multiple determination in respect of the assets, sales, and
employment equations are respectively 0.5358, 0.5066 and
0.4183.

The relationship between adjusted profitability and growth was
also tested using nonparametric statistics, and the results of
this are presented below.

TABLE 4.13 Nonparametric Analysis of Size, Profitability and
            Growth

	Fisher's Exact	Mann-Whitney	Random-isation	Rho
	D	U	t	
Opening Size and Growth:				
Assets	2	19	0.4151	0.0983
Sales	5	24	0.2500	-0.0250
Employment	2	20	0.1351	-0.0716
Growth and Profitability:				
Assets	0*	8*	2.4878**	0.6130**
Sales	2*	7*	3.4643***	0.6857***
Employment	0**	8*	2.4444*	0.5760**

*significant at 10%; **significant at 5% ***significant at 1%.

To answer the question relating to the persistency of growth
over the whole period, and also to find out whether there
was evidence of a pattern of growth within it, the growth
experience of the 15 firms in respect of assets, sales and
employment was broken down into the two subperiods 1968-1972
and 1973-1977. (In the case of employment, the absence of
1967 data meant that the two subperiods were 1969-1972 and
1973-1977.) The first task was to compare the (unweighted)
average annual growth rates in the two subperiods; and the
results of this, in terms of both parametric and nonparametric tests, are presented below in Table 4.14.

TABLE 4.14   Comparison of Average Annual Growth Rates in Two
             Subperiods

| | Average Annual Growth Rate | | t^{**} | t | Prob.Under H_o | |
	1968-72	1973-77			Sign Test	Wil-coxon (T)
Assets	-2.1	-2.2	0.0387	0.0238	1.000	47
Sales	2.8	-1.3	2.7333***	1.6400	0.118	17***
Employment*	-3.6	-1.1	1.0909	0.8621	1.000	44

*   1969-72 and 1973-77
**   the t test used was one which treated the two subperiod
       averages for each firm as 15 paired observations, see
       Daniel, W.W. and J.C. Terrell (1975).
***   significant at 5% (two tailed).

From the above table it is clear that, with the exception of
both the parametric and nonparametric paired tests in respect
of sales data, there was no change in the growth performance
of this group of firms over the two subperiods. What is
interesting to note is the divergence of the data within the
columns of the table, with regard to growth rates. It would
appear that the industry's annual rate of decline of asset
volume continued at just over 2% for the whole period, but
that the rate of decline of labour slowed down somewhat.
Sales, on the other hand, expanded in real terms by 2.8% per
annum 1968-1972, while asset and labour inputs were falling,
but turned round to decline by 1.3% per annum 1973-1977, a
rate of decline lying somewhere between that of assets and
employment in the industry.

Given the lack of clear change in the growth rates over the
two subperiods, a further question to be asked is, did the
relative positions of the firms to one another in respect of
their growth rates alter between the two subperiods? The
answer is given in Table 4.15 below in terms of the correl-

ation of the ranks of growth over the two subperiods.

TABLE 4.15   Spearman Rank Correlation Coefficients of Subperiod
             Growth Rates

	Rho	t
Assets	O.3643	1.4104
Sales	O.5893	2.6300*
Employment	O.3220	1.2263

   * significant at 5% (two-tailed).

Table 4.15 suggests that, with the exception of sales growth,
there was some disruption to the previous (1968-72) rank
order of growth in the following (1973-77) subperiod. This is
in contrast to the experience with regard to profit performance (see p.109 above). However, sales growth was an exception to this: firms which did relatively well (or badly)
in the former subperiod performed relatively well (or badly)
in the latter. It may be that the sales growth data is the
most reliable in this instance, as a change in the ranks of
asset or employment growth might merely indicate a movement
from labour- to capital-intensive technology by different
firms at different times. Firms making this change in, say,
subperiod 1 would rank highly on asset growth relative to
others; but, having completed the changeover, might be expected to rank below others in the following subperiod. Thus the
overall conclusion on the stability of growth in the two subperiods is that, as in the case of profitability, there was no
disruption among the firms in terms of growth.

The final piece of analysis carried out here is to test the
strength of the relationship between growth in the former subperiod (as the independent variable) and growth in the latter.
This was done by means of linear regression, and the results
are tabulated in Table 4.16 below.

TABLE 4.16   Linear Regression of Subperiod Growth Rates

	Constant	b	t	R^2	DW**
Assets	-1.5	O.3190	1.4770	0.1437	1.1170≠
Sales	-2.8	O.5369	2.7157*	0.3620	1.2927≠
Employment	-O.4	O.2141	1.1706	0.0954	1.9884

* significant at 2%;   ** not significant at 10%;
≠ indeterminate.

Once again the sales data stand out as indicating in this

case a fairly strong positive relationship between growth in
the two subperiods. However, the coefficient of determination
is fairly low, indicating only a modest degree of explanatoriness.

A summary of the findings with regard to growth for our group
of firms over the period 1968-1977 is as follows. The results
apply in respect of growth in terms of assets, sales and
employment, and to parametric as well as nonparametric tests,
unless otherwise stated.

1. (Opening) size had no impact upon the 10-year
   growth record of the firms.

2. In particular, a specific test for the existence
   of Gibrat's Law (Table 4.10) suggested quite
   clearly that the proportional rate of growth
   for firms over the period was independent of
   firm size.

3. The relationship between 10-year average profits
   and 10-year average growth was highly significant. That is, firms which were generally over
   the period profitable also exhibited high growth
   rates. The point should, however, be made that
   such cross-sectional statistics did not allow one
   to arrive at clear causal relationships between,
   say, profitability and growth.

4. In respect of asset and employment data, there
   were no significant changes in the growth rates
   between the two subperiods 1968-1972 and 1973-
   1977. The reduction in the rate of growth of
   sales between the two subperiods was significant.

5. Testing for relative consistency of performance
   by measuring Rho in respect of growth rates for
   the two subperiods, only in respect of sales
   would it appear that the firms performed consistently relative to one another.

6. Finally, the growth rates in the latter subperiod
   were regarded as the outcome of growth in the
   former (Table 4.16). Again only in the case of
   sales was there a significant (positive) relationship between growth performance in the two subperiods.

EMPLOYMENT AND LABOUR PRODUCTIVITY

Since it is a vital factor of production, any study of the
performance of an industry must make reference to its use of
labour. The reduction in the total labour force in this
industry is only the most obvious statistic in this area.
More detailed work is required to arrive at a view on the
industry's use of labour in total.

So far as the Dundee jute industry is concerned, some of the
more recent history of labour usage appears to have been shaped
by much more distant events, including a rather harsh and rem-
ote relationship between the "jute barons" of the nineteenth
century and their largely unskilled workforce. The dominance
of the jute industry in the city of Dundee has not helped
matters, for unemployment in the jute industry has meant hard
times for the city as a whole. The historical significance of
jute employment in the area may be understood from the
following data relating to textile employment. That this was
largely accounted for by the jute industry may be gathered from
the further estimate that in 1924 50% of the "workers in the
city (Dundee)" were employed in the jute industry (Times,
1952).

TABLE 4.17 Textile Employment in Dundee as a Proportion of
            Total

1881	49%
1911	48
1931	41
1951	23
1961	18

Source: Carstairs, A.M. (1968). The nature of diversification
         of employment in Dundee". In S.J. Jones (Ed.),
         Dundee and District. British Association, Dundee,
         pp.320 and 329.

A further feature of employment in the industry has been the
past incidence of unemployment and low wages. Lenman (1977,
p.201) in his recent economic history of Scotland speaks of
the scale on which men from Dundee joined the armed forces in
1914 as "a glowing tribute to the recruiting effect of heavy
unemployment and grinding poverty", and instances with regard
to the times of depression that in July 1932 there were 37,000
unemployed jute workers in Dundee (Lenman, 1977, p.219).
Again the Report of the 1948 Board of Trade Working Party
(p.9), having spoken of the massive unemployment in the jute
industry in the 1930's, summed up:

>"Short time, low wages, idle mills and spells of
>prolonged unemployment were the lot of the jute
>workers, and since the industry ... was the major
>one in Dundee, the depression laid a heavy hand
>on the city and her people suffered acutely."

That this view was not unduly coloured by proximity to the
time may be gathered from more recent reference (Southgate,
1968) to Dundee as "a city in which industrial relations were
poisoned by the low wages of the (jute) industry, by the
connection of the employers with the competing jute industry
of India and by devastating unemployment between the wars".
What has also to be remembered in this context is that in the
past the skilled work in the jute industry was predominantly
carried out by female labour. For example Walker in his historical study points out that in 1885 females in the jute
industry outnumbered males by three to one; and that with
women carrying out the "prestige" tasks in the industry they
had created for themselves a separate "aristocracy of labour".
It was reportedly said that in Dundee the women worked while
the men stayed at home; and employers had a reputation for
taking on boys for unskilled work and paying them off when
they were old enough to receive an adult wage. With regard
to changes in the overall level of employment in the industry,
the jute trade lost a large part of its labour force during
World War II. Employment in Dundee fell from about 26,000 in
1939 to 11,000 in 1945. Figures relating to Dundee and district show an expansion of this latter figure to around 13,000
in 1950. Appendix Table 4.1 contains a consistent set of
data from 1948 to 1977 relating to actual employment in the
industry - i.e. employees or insured persons in employment.
From the data one can discern two things clearly: the fall in
the total number of persons employed, especially since 1966;
and also the changed ratio of male to female workers. The
reduction in male employment over the whole period 1948-1977
was 33%, while in the case of females it was 78%. This divergence is again reflected in the change in the ratio of females
to males in the industry from 1.6:1 in 1948 to 0.5:1 in 1977.
Unemployment data are more difficult to interpret as they
represent neither purely a stock of unemployed nor a flow into
and out of the jute industry. (Employees unemployed in the
jute industry may leave this category to become employed in
other industries.) From a consideration of unemployment and
industry output data, however, one could suggest that whereas
in earlier periods temporary unemployment might later be
reduced by reabsorbing labour into the industry, from the mid
1960's onwards there was a final shedding of labour by the
industry at a considerable rate.

The impact of the general labour situation in more recent
decades has been to make "going into the mill" an unattractive
prospect even for more skilled workers; and this has influenced the investment and location decisions of firms in the
industry in the period since 1945. A major problem for the
industry in the immediate post-war period, however, was that
of a shortage of labour. This was brought about by a combination of a reluctance of previous employees to return to the
industry after war service, and a lack of new recruits influenced by the image of pre-war unemployment. To these
negative supply factors was added the competition for semi-
skilled male and female labour which was at that time being
offered to the industry by firms in the light-engineering
sector which were establishing themselves on the new
industrial estates around Dundee's northern perimeter. Wage
and labour competition from this source has in fact been a
frequent talking point in the jute industry for the past
thirty years. The lack of suitable labour was put forward by
the industry in the 1950's as a major reason for not being
able to meet demand. It has also been said to have influenced
decisions on capital-intensive modernisation schemes. Most of
such new investment was "costed" on the basis of double shift
working so as to write off the new plant over as large an output as possible. Where such double shift working was not
possible due to labour shortage, it is possible that there was
a reduced incentive to new capital investment.

In more recent times, although the total workforce of the
industry has declined rapidly, shortage of suitable labour
has nonetheless figured in discussions within the industry.
The Financial Times (2.4.59 and 15.2.60), for example,
described labour shortages in the late 1950's as "acute", and
spoke of "a great scarcity of workers for both spinning and
weaving". It has been held that those firms wishing to expand
output were forced to acquire other businesses rather than
install more machinery in their own plants, in order to
acquire additional labour. More recently, and with the rapid
falling away of demand for jute goods, the industry has become
more aware of what is openly admitted to be a declining
standard of quality of new recruits. Although polypropylene
processing does demand a higher standard of operative labour,
it is a much more capital intensive manufacturing process;
and in this way firms have reduced their dependence upon
labour. A further policy has been one of geographical diversification; and much of the expansion in recent years by
Dundee-based firms has been in Fife, new industrial estates
in South Wales and West Scotland, and even in the industrial
Midlands. In these locations the firms may be seeking a more
skilled or adaptable labour force, more generous Government

assistance, or sites better placed for marketing and transport of raw materials and finished goods.

It is not easy to measure labour productivity directly from available aggregated data. Isolated figures, however, suggest that the industry has succeeded in improving its performance in this direction. It was pointed out in the early 1950's, for example, that while employment had declined by 40% compared with the pre-war situation, output in the industry was only 25% below the 1939 figure (Financial Times, 29.3.54). The British Jute Trade Federal Council was reported as claiming in 1960 that spinning output per worker had increased by 40% over the previous decade (Financial Times 15.6.60); the Financial Times (30.7.62) further reported that in the previous 13 years output per man in yarn spinning had increased by 78%, with a comparable figure for spinning, weaving and finishing of 56%; while the Restrictive Practices Court was informed in 1963 that in jute spinning the number of workers per ton per week had fallen from 3.63 in 1949 to 2.16 in 1961, and that similar improvements had been made in weaving (L.R.4R.P.). Finally, the following index was published by the British Jute Trade Federal Council.

TABLE 4.18   Index of Productivity in Jute Spinning
             (1949 = 100)

Year	Index	Year	Index
1950	108	1957	140
1951	113	1958	152
1952	114	1959	153
1953	125	1960	160
1954	126	1961	168
1955	133	1962	169
1956	138	1963	170

Source: B.J.T.F.C. quoted in Financial Times, 14th December 1964.

Using the data in Appendix Table 2.1 to Chapter 2 and Appendix Table 4.1, the following figures emerge from an analysis of output and employment divided into three sub-periods representing some stability after World War II (1945-1960), the beginnings of decline (1961-1969), and the collapse of the traditional jute industry (1970-1977).

TABLE 4.19   Changes in Employment and Jute Spinning and
             Weaving Output

	Change in Employment %	Changes in Output %	
		Yarn	Cloth
1948-60	-15.2	+41.4	+39.4
1961-69	- 8.9	- 8.1	-24.6
1970-77	-32.8	-46.5	-66.3

Source: Annual Abstract of Statistics. H.M.S.O., London.

The results of this type of analysis for the first subperiod
are quite unequivocal. Between 1948 and 1960 employment in
the industry fell by 15.2% while output of yarn and of cloth
rose by 41.4% and 39.4% respectively. Over the period of
contraction of output from 1961-69 the reduction in employment, though marginally ahead of that in yarn, was well
behind that of cloth. The pattern of data in respect of the
most recent figure suggest a falling off in labour productivity; although by this stage there may have begun to be a
lack of correspondence between those employees classed as
"jute" and those who were fully and solely employed in
spinning or weaving jute as opposed to other fibres.

A less direct measure is to compare raw jute consumption per
employee over the period 1948 to date, as a measure of the
quantity of material processed per employee.

TABLE 4.20   Raw Jute Consumption per Employee (tonnes per
             annum)

1948	5.00	1958	7.65	1968	7.29
1949	5.23	1959	8.12	1969	7.00
1950	6.19	1960	8.22	1970	7.29
1951	6.05	1961	6.91	1971	7.54
1952	6.35	1962	7.51	1972	8.21
1953	6.64	1963	7.92	1973	7.66
1954	6.62	1964	7.58	1974	6.31
1955	7.35	1965	7.37	1975	6.48
1956	7.44	1966	7.16	1976	6.28
1957	7.47	1967	7.44	1977	5.79

Source: Annual Abstract of Statistics. H.M.S.O., London.

These figures suggest an improvement in labour productivity
from 1948 which was sustained until 1960. Thereafter performance appears to have slipped somewhat; although it has remained above the levels of the mid 1950's, and once again may
be understated if some employees not wholly engaged in jute
spinning and weaving are included in the industry. This

pattern is emphasised if one compares the data for jute with
labour productivity indices for U.K. manufacturing industry
as a whole and in respect of the Textiles sector. The raw
data for this are set out in Appendix Table 4.4 and comprise
figures for output per person employed in index form taken
from British Labour Statistics together with the original
data from Table 4.20 above in index form. The conclusion
one arrives at from a comparison of the first two index
number columns in Appendix Table 4.4 is that whereas productivity in jute more than kept pace with that in manufacturing
industry as a whole from 1950 until 1960, the former compares
very unfavourably with the latter from this period onwards,
especially during the late 1960's and the 1970's. A comparison with Textiles is only possible from 1963 onwards in terms
of data availability, but again in terms of this closer comparison jute shows up very badly.

Wages in the jute industry are determined by two Joint
Industrial Councils (J.I.C.'s): one covering Dundee employers
and unions, the other non-Dundee (basically Forfar and Kirriemuir) representatives. The J.I.C's took over from the Jute
Wages Council in 1970, and appear to have inherited a system
of fairly stable industrial relations. Data on jute industry
wages are not available prior to 1960; but for the period
1960-1977 some comparison can be made with manual workers'
earnings in manufacturing industry as a whole. The following
figures are derived from Appendix Tables 4.2 and 4.3

TABLE 4.21   Hourly Earnings (£)

	Jute Industry		Mfg.Industry		Ratios: Jute Industry/Mfg. Men	Ratios: Jute Industry/Mfg. Women	Ratios: Jute Industry: Men/Women
	Men	Women	Men	Women			
1960	0.25	0.17	0.32	0.18	0.78	0.94	1.47
1961	0.26	0.18	0.34	0.19	0.76	0.95	1.44
1962	0.28	0.20	0.35	0.20	0.80	1.00	1.40
1963	0.29	0.20	0.37	0.21	0.78	0.95	1.45
1964	0.31	0.22	0.40	0.23	0.78	0.96	1.41
1965	0.33	0.23	0.44	0.25	0.75	0.92	1.43
1966	0.36	0.25	0.46	0.26	0.78	0.96	1.44
1967	0.40	0.27	0.48	0.28	0.83	0.96	1.48
1968	0.42	0.29	0.52	0.30	0.81	0.97	1.45
1969	0.48	0.33	0.56	0.32	0.86	1.03	1.45
1970	0.53	0.33	0.64	0.37	0.83	0.89	1.61
1971	0.56	0.41	0.72	0.42	0.77	0.98	1.37
1972	0.67	0.48	0.82	0.49	0.82	0.98	1.40
1973	0.77	0.58	0.93	0.56	0.83	1.04	1.33
1974	0.93	0.74	1.12	0.73	0.83	1.01	1.26
1975	1.18	0.96	1.40	0.93	0.84	1.03	1.23
1976	1.27	1.13	1.56	1.09	0.81	1.04	1.12
1977	1.32	1.17	1.62	1.13	0.81	1.04	1.13

Source: Appendix Tables 4.2 and 4.3.

Taking male employment first - which rose from 51% to 67% of the total over the period 1960-1977 - weekly hours worked in the jute industry do not appear to have differed significantly from those in manufacturing industry as a whole. Earnings per hour in jute have, however, remained below those in manufacturing. The "discount" was 22% in 1960, and had only narrowed to 19% in 1977. This slight narrowing is reflected in the ratio of 1977 hourly rates to those for 1960: 5.28 for jute, 5.06 for manufacturing. Use of such ratios shows that during the rapid change in hourly rates in 1974-1975 the premium of manufacturing wages over jute earnings was narrowed somewhat. Thus, although wages in the jute industry have remained lower than for manufacturing industry as a whole, there has been no increased deterioration by this comparison.

With regard to female earnings the comparative situation is very different. Over the period 1960-1977 women too in jute manufacturing have increased their hourly earnings at a faster rate than those in manufacturing in general; ratios of 1960 to 1977 female hourly rates being 6.88 for jute and 6.28 for manufacturing industry. However, for women in the jute industry this represents an improvement from a situation in which they were earning slightly less per hour (a discount of

5.5% off the figure for manufacturing) to one in 1977 in
which they earned a premium of 3.5%. This has been accompanied by a diminishing gap between male and female hourly
earnings. In 1960 the ratio of female to male hourly earnings
was 0.68 for jute and 0.56 for manufacturing. In 1977 the
respective figures were 0.89 and 0.70. Women in the jute
industry have thus significantly improved their earnings
position; and this does not appear to have been as a result
of overtime working.

In general, therefore, income from employment in the jute
industry have kept pace with the general rise in earnings in
manufacturing industry; and figures for weekly hours worked
suggest that this reflects underlying basic wage rates rather
than excessive overtime at premium rates. The data also
suggest that there are no grounds for the hypothesis that the
continued existence of the U.K. jute industry, or a reduction
in its rate of decline, has been based upon low wages, or a
failure of those wages to keep pace with industry in general.

Finally, it is worth commenting on the generally good industrial relations that have existed in this market. After 1945
the industry appears to have adopted a new approach to
employee relations: partly the result of a new, younger group
of owners emerging among the larger businesses, and partly
arising from a realisation that, following demobilisation, the
jute industry might not attract back to it all of those who
left in 1939 and 1940. To this last factor was soon to be
added competition for semi-skilled labour from new, often
American, businesses established on Dundee's recently created
industrial estates established around its northern perimeter.
It was, in fact, a relative labour shortage in the industry
which stimulated both increased mechanisation and the introduction of work study and logical re-deployment of labour.
This work was initiated within the industry (one of the
first, indeed, to do so) but was often carried out by independent firms of consultants. The result was a new wage
system introduced in 1952 based upon job evaluation, and
improved labour productivity referred to above. Indeed the
situation called forth a "surprised" reaction from two
observers (Carter and Williams, 1957, p.225) that "the
employment of industrial consultants has become almost a
commonplace throughout an industry where the tradition has
long been one of conservatism on the part of both employers
and employees". This changed attitude meant not only a
fairly rapid acceptance by workers of job evaluation schemes
etc., but was also accompanied by a genuine concern for
employees on the part of mill and factory owners. For example,
an estimated two thirds of establishments in the industry had

a personnel officer by the mid 1950's.

Over the restricted time period of 1968-1977 it was possible
to use data on real sales and employment to measure labour
productivity at the individual firm level. This approach
could only be adopted over this shorter period because of
the lack of earlier data. The figure calculated was that of
sales at constant 1967 terms per employee per annum. Throughout this study in respect of data derived from company reports,
figures relating to sales rather than output have been used
even where, for example in analysing labour productivity, one
might have expected to be able to analyse the behaviour of
output per head. Sales data have been used not only because
they are the data explicitly presented in company annual
reports but because the translation of sales into output by
means of adjusting for the building up or running down of
stocks is not possible on the basis of published data.
Company annual reports do contain data on stocks. These data
however relate to stocks of raw materials, work in progress
and finished goods, whereas it is only the last category
which concerns us. Moreover, the stock figure is usually
presented in company accounts combined with debtors - another
current asset. Over a 10-year period it is not considered
that any serious error is likely to arise in using sales data
in this way as a surrogate for output.

The data, which were available in respect of 15 firms, are
not perfect. On the employment side, part-time staff in the
denominator may distort the figure; although it is considered that this is not likely to be a serious source of error
because of the relatively small number of those involved.
More contentious is the correction for inflation used to
produce "real" turnover data over the period. The actual
sales figures in each year for each of the 15 firms were re-
stated on the basis of 1967 prices using the output wholesale prices index (Textiles). It was hoped by such means to
indicate the increase or decrease in sales per annum, correct-
ing for the trend of price increases.

The results of the analysis indicate, firstly, a surprising
range of averages for sales per employee over the 10-year
period. These ranged from £2,040 from a small synthetic
spinning firm to £13,170 for a large diversified company
(both figures in 1967 terms). The unweighted average for
the 15 firms in index form over the period was as follows.

TABLE 4.22   Sales per Employee at Constant Prices (1968 = 100)

	15-Firm Average	U.K. Manufacturing Industry*
1968	100	100
1969	102	102
1970	108	104
1971	115	106
1972	130	113
1973	131	121
1974	127	119
1975	141	117
1976	140	122
1977	125	122

* The figure here is the volume index of manufacturing output
  for the U.K. divided in each year by the total number of
  employees in employment in manufacturing industry and converted into index form 1968 = 100. The source for the data
  is British Labour Statistics (H.M.S.O., London). See
  Appendix Table 4.4.

For our industry the data indicate a considerable rise in
labour productivity from 1968 up to the mid 1970's. These
data are, however, difficult to interpret, especially when
compared with those for manufacturing industry as a whole.
In particular, one would suspect that because the wholesale
price index for Textiles as a whole has probably lagged behind a more accurate price index for the sales or output of
our firms their output has in real terms been overstated.

The company accounts data discussed immediately above were
also used to try to establish "causes" of the variation in
the level of labour productivity within our 15-firm population. Average size was the first independent variable chosen
for the linear regression analysis.

TABLE 4.23   Linear Relationship of Firm Size and Labour
             Productivity

Dependent variable: 10-year average real sales per employee

Average Size Measure	Constant	b	t	R^2	DW***
Assets	3.13	0.00058	6.7498**	0.7780	1.8101
Sales	3.06	0.00026	6.3053**	0.7536	1.7635
Employment	3.34	0.00019	2.1432*	0.2611	2.0170

* significant at 10% ** significant at 0.1%; *** not significant at 10%.

The unmistakable conclusion is that size, as measured by
assets or sales, is very clearly associated with labour
productivity. Although the t statistic in respect of labour
as a size measure was also significant (at 10%), by comparison with alternative size measures labour performed poorly,
as is clearly reflected in the respective coefficients of
determination. Another possible influence upon labour productivity is growth, on the grounds that growth yields benefits
in terms of learning, or that is gives access to economies of
scale. The former effect is simply one aspect of the general
hypothesis regarding growth and productivity known as
Verdoorn's Law (George, 1971).

TABLE 4.24   Linear Relationship of Growth and Labour Productivity

Dependent variable: as in Table 4.23

Growth Measure	Constant	b	t	R^2	DW**
Assets	4.72	0.11657	1.5121	0.1496	2.0590
Sales	4.31	0.17076	1.4471	0.1386	1.9727
Employment	4.94	0.22183	1.9545*	0.2272	1.8872

* significant at 10%;   ** not significant at 10%.

In respect of growth, the degree of explanation of variations
in labour productivity is low compared with size. Furthermore, the roles of the individual size or growth variables
were reversed with regard to the parametric test. Growth of
employment is significant in terms of the t statistic at 10%;
although even here the coefficient of determination is low
compared with those in Table 4.23.

Finally, on a bivariate basis, capital per employee was
chosen as an independent variable; and this was measured as
net assets (from company balance sheets) per employee in real
terms, assets being converted into 1967 terms by reference to
Current Cost Accounting indices for the appropriate Minimum
List Heading. The results of the linear regression indicate
the importance of this variable, which on a bivariate basis
is more significant than firm size.

TABLE 4.25   Linear Regression of Capital Intensiveness and
Labour Productivity

Dependent variable: as in Table 4.23

Constant	b	t	R^2	DW**
0.81	1.96390	9.4237*	0.8723	1.2627

*significant at 0.1%;   ** not significant at 10%, within
indeterminate range.

The relative importance of size, growth and capital intensiveness can be seen from the multivariate analysis, including
partial correlation coefficients.

TABLE 4.26   Linear Regression of Size, Growth, Capital
             Intensiveness and Labour Productivity

Dependent variable: as in Table 4.23

Independent Variable	Constant	b*	t	r*
Size (Sales)	1.79	0.00023	1.8256**	0.4823
Growth (Employment)		0.04772	1.6013	0.4347
Capital Intensiveness		1.19984	2.7955***	0.6445

Multiple R^2 = 0.9101   F = 34.14****   DW = 1.8818 (not significant at 10%).

* partial coefficients; significance levels: ** 10%,
  *** 5%, **** 1%.

The conclusion in respect of our group of firms on the average
level of labour productivity is that capital intensiveness and
average size (in terms of assets and sales) are very significant determinants. Growth appears to offer much less of an
explanation, although in the case of growth of employment the
coefficient of determination was 0.2272. These relative
contributions are highlighted in Table 4.26 above.

With regard to growth of labour productivity over the period
1969-1977, this was measured as the average annual rate of
growth of sales per employee.

TABLE 4.27   Linear Regression of Firm Size and Labour
             Productivity Growth

Dependent variable: 9-year average annual rate of growth of
                     labour productivity

Average Size Measure	Constant	b	t	R^2	DW*
Assets	3.2	-0.00018	1.7615	0.1927	1.5569
Sales	3.2	-0.00008	1.6642	0.1756	1.5311
Employment	3.1	-0.00037	0.9418	0.0639	1.4416

* not significant at 10%.

None of the results in Table 4.27 is significant; although it
is interesting to note the negative sign of the b coefficient
with respect to all of the size measures. This would suggest,
although it must be stressed that the results are not statistically significant, that over this period small firms have

demonstrated higher rates of labour productivity growth than
larger ones.

The results of the linear regression of the growth of firms
and the growth of labour productivity are presented in Table
4.28 below.

TABLE 4.28   Linear Regression of Firm Growth and Labour
             Productivity Growth

Dependent variable: as in Table 4.27.

Growth Measure	Constant	b	t	R^2	DW*
Assets	2.8	0.02643	0.5046	0.0192	1.6147
Sales	2.7	0.04929	0.6218	0.0289	1.4161
Employment	2.7	-0.03810	0.4707	0.0168	1.6078

* not significant at 10%.

Surprisingly, again none of the results is significant; and
in the case of growth of employment, although it must be
stressed again that the results are not significant, it would
appear that firms which expanded employment less rapidly experienced higher rates of growth in labour productivity.

TABLE 4.29   Linear Relationship of Capital Intensiveness and
             Growth of Labour Productivity

Dependent variable: as in Table 4.32

Capital Intensiveness	Constant	b	t	R^2	DW*
Average	3.6	-0.46508	1.6322	0.1223	2.3188
Growth	2.9	0.10075	1.1685	0.0951	2.1246

* not significant at 10%.

Taking the cross-sectional figures on capital intensiveness -
i.e. the average data for each firm over the period 1968-
1977, and the corresponding average growth rate 1969-1977 -
again none of the results is significant (at 10%). Within
these limitations it nonetheless appears that more highly
capital intensive firms had lower rates of growth of labour
productivity than less capital intensive. Increases in
capital intensiveness over the period may, however, have
been associated with faster rates of growth in labour productivity.

The use of sales per person as a measure of labour productivity is not of course ideal. It is true that unless there
were violent fluctuations in the level of stocks held then

sales and (gross) output should strongly coincide as measures
of production and productivity. However, the extent of vertical integration within our group of firms varies quite considerably as we saw in Chapter 2. Low levels of vertical
integration obviously overstate the labour productivity of a
firm relative to that of a business which is highly vertically
integrated when sales per person is used as a measure of
labour productivity. Moreover, the extent of vertical integration may be related to factors such as firm size used as
independent variables in seeking to explain differences in
labour productivity among firms. The data in Appendix Table
4.9 indicate a significant negative relationship between firm
size and the extent of vertical integration. In order to
avoid this problem the regressions in Tables 4.23-4.29 were
recalculated using value added per employee as a measure of
labour productivity.

Briefly comparing the company-accounts-based labour productivity analysis on a sales and value added basis one finds that
the effect of using the latter basis in a bivariate regression
is somewhat to mute the influence of firm size on labour
productivity. In the case of the impact of firm growth on
labour productivity, measuring the latter on a value added
basis greatly increases the impact of growth on average labour
productivity. The former change is particularly explained by
the relationship between size and the average index of vertical
integration revealed in Appendix Table 4.9. The low degree of
explanatoriness of firm size, growth and capital intensiveness
with regard to labour productivity growth was not changed when
the latter was measured on a value-added basis.

It is believed that value added per employee is a more correct
measure of labour productivity, and this has therefore been
used in conducting the nonparametric tests in this area. The
results of these tests are reported in Table 4.30 below.

TABLE 4.30   Nonparametric Tests on Labour Productivity on
             Value-Added Basis

		Fisher's Exact D	Mann-Whitney U	Random-isation t	Rho

Average Labour Productivity:

Average size:	Sales	0**	8**	1.6957	0.6464***
	Assets	0	6***	1.9048	0.6536***
	Value Added	0	12	1.5600	0.6750***
	Employment	0	12	1.5600	0.4808*
Growth :	Sales	2	13	1.7391	0.6643***
	Assets	1	11**	1.9048	0.7668***
	Value Added	1	13	1.5455	0.6179**
	Employment	1	15	1.5000	0.6810***
Average capital intensiveness		0	8***	2.3000**	0.8382***

Labour Productivity Growth:

Average size:	Sales	2	28	0.6470	-0.0966
	Assets	1	19	0.1111	-0.0823
	Value Added	0	12	1.2632	-0.0662
	Employment	0	12	1.2632	-0.0358
Growth :	Sales	1	25	0.1667	-0.2469
	Assets	1	23	0.2778	-0.0976
	Value Added	1	20	0.1667	0.1592
	Employment	1	19	0.1579	-0.2310
Capital intensiveness growth		1	14	0.1053	0.0161

Significance levels: *10%,   **5%,   ***1%.

The conclusions on employment and labour productivity in the
industry are as follows.

1.   There was a rapid decline in the total number
     of employees in employment in the industry from
     1967 onwards.

2.   This decline was particularly rapid among
     female rather than male employees, and this is
     reflected in the changed ratio of female to
     male employees in the industry.   This is a
     reflection of changes in the technology of the
     industry.

3.   For male employment, although earnings per hour
     are still around 20% less than those of U.K.

manufacturing industry as a whole, this "discount" has not changed significantly over the past decade and a half.

4.   For female employees there has been a considerable increase in hourly earnings since 1960. This increase has brought these earnings in jute much more into line with male earnings (although the "female discount" is still in excess of 10%), and has taken jute industry females from a slight discount compared with manufacturing industry as regards hourly earnings in 1960 to a premium position of around 4% in 1977.

5.   As regards labour productivity, there appear to have been considerable strides made in this area from 1948 onwards, the period 1948-1960 being a particularly outstanding one. Since 1960 progress has been less obvious - see Tables 4.19 and 4.20 - suggesting some relationship between industry growth and productivity.

6.   Over the more restricted period 1968-1977 company accounting data suggest that the average level of labour productivity was significantly influenced by average firm size, growth and capital intensiveness.

7.   As regards growth of labour productivity 1969-1977, no clear picture emerges from the analysis of our population of firms. Neither firm size nor growth were significant independent variables, nor was capital intensiveness.

INVESTMENT AND MODERNISATION

An important aspect of any industry's performance is the extent to which it has invested in new capital equipment in order to keep its plant up to date and to maintain itself at the forefront of technology. The first approach to examining this issue in the jute industry was to try to construct a time series of total new capital investment since 1945. The data are not entirely satisfactory since they may be based upon different concepts of new investment. Census data, for example, consider investment as acquisitions less disposals, while business people tend to think in gross (acquisitions only) terms. On the other hand Census data include vehicles as well as plant and buildings, whereas industry estimates will exclude the first category. The data for total new

capital investment since 1945, and for annual new investment
in each year are given in Appendix Table 4.5.

The new investment data were gathered from a variety of
sources, not all of which adopted consistent definitions.
From these, however, it was possible to graph total investment from 1945 to 1977, and read off the growth data for individual years. The results of this exercise are shown in
Appendix Table 4.5 and in graphical form in the following
Appendix Tables. Column 1 shows the total, and column 2 the
annual investment at each date. These data are expressed in
current prices; and although a particular pattern emerges
over certain time periods it is possible that this could have
been influenced by changing rates of inflation. Fortunately,
a by-product of recent concern over inflation accounting has
been the publication of a series of price indices of, inter
alia, plant and equipment in various industries, running from
1956 to the present time. The appropriate category of these
has been used to inflate or deflate the data in column 2
into a common value basis (1970 = 100). This has enabled one
to produce in column 4 a series of annual investment figures
at 1970 prices. For the period 1948 to 1955 the current
price levels for investment have been inflated by an All
Industries capital expenditure (machinery and plant) index
using the same source as the more disaggregated index and
linking the two sets of indices at 1956. No constant price
data are available for the period 1945-47, but even the current
data are largely estimates up to 1950, so that only by that
latter date do we have an accurate idea of the level of investment in the immediate post-war period.

The graph of total new investment in current values (Appendix
Table 4.6) suggests that from 1945 to the later 1950's expendi-
tures were rising at an increased rate. This rate of new
investment appears to have slowed down for the first part of
the 1960's, but accelerated from around 1964 onwards. It
should, of course, be borne in mind that in respect of data
stated in current terms an upsurge in the rate of general
inflation in the economy could create the impression of increased capital spending, which was nonetheless in real terms
fairly static. Thus the restatement of annual levels of
investment in constant price terms gives a much more accurate
indication of events. These are presented in Appendix Table
4.7, with 3-year moving averages in dotted lines.

Despite the problem of sources of data, the figures reflect
what discussions within the industry also suggest. The period
following 1945, during which Control and the trading agreements were of significance in the industry, was one of con-

siderable new capital spending. This was the era in which
individual electric motors (rather than single motors and
multiple drive belts) were introduced into weaving. Circular
looms (for bag making) and automatic cop loading were also
brought into use in weaving. On the spinning side considerable investment was made in automatic spindles; and by the
early 1960's the industry was based entirely upon high-speed
or "sliver" spindles. Indeed for 1960 the Financial Times
(15.6.60) was able to report that only 3% of the spinning
machinery was of the "old type" (i.e. mule spinning), while
nearly half of the looms were automatic. In addition to these
technical innovations, considerable improvements were being
made over this period in plant layout, often in new factory
buildings. Indeed the Financial Times had been able to comment
by the mid 1950's (29.3.54) that "the British (jute) industry
today must be classed as one of the most up-to-date textile
industries in the world". Even by the early 1960's, when the
jute industry had certainly passed the peak of its new capital
expansion rate, the same newspaper (18.11.63) considered that
"Jute has for its size been one of the British industries most
conspicuous in modernising plant and equipment".

When asked about the forces behind the spate of new investment
in the industry for the decade and a half after 1945 members
of the industry have placed some emphasis on the protective
environment of Control and the trade pricing agreements. These
gave the industry confidence in a more stable future demand,
at least with regard to Indian competition. In respect of the
impact of the trading agreements, it was argued by the industry
(Robertson, 1962):

> "There is no other traditional textile industry
> which has re-equipped itself to so considerable
> an extent. It is virtually certain that only a
> very small proportion of this re-equipment would
> have been undertaken had there not been a general
> assurance of economic stability and of future
> prospects conferred by the combined structure of
> protection (i.e. Control) and of the Seven
> Registered Agreements. ... If the agreements were
> discontinued and protection terminated or rendered
> inoperative, capital expenditure in the jute
> industry would be reduced to a small fraction of
> its present level. In consequence there would be
> reduced prospect of any future productivity im-
> provement by way of new machinery, and future
> wage increases would fall very largely upon the
> final price of the product."

This incentive effect was also embodied in the conclusion of
an academic study of the conditions for technical progress in
industry (Carter and Williams, 1954, p.187). Thus,

> "In the jute industry, the greater security given
> by import controls and by Government purchasing has
> freed managers from the immediate struggle for
> existence, and they have been able to give attention
> to the introduction of new equipment which had been
> developed in other industries."

These same authors also suggest that a further benefit to the
industry from Control's operations was the taking over by
Control of the risk and financial cost of stockholding of raw
jute. This produced a situation in which firms had additional
funds with which to finance new investment in plant etc.

What one cannot judge from the statistics and general dis-
cussion on capital investment and its causes is the rate at
which new ideas have been adopted by the industry as a whole
relative to what they might have been, and the speed and
method by which such innovations were adopted across the
industry. Some firms have evidently re-equipped substantially
and frequently, others have continued to use very old jute
machinery, and even continue to weave mixtures or polypropylene on jute looms. Sidlaw, for example, spent around
£1,200,000 in 1967 in modernising its jute spinning capacity
(Dundee Chamber, Dec.1967, p.595), while even quite small
firms have spent considerable sums merely installing polypropylene weaving equipment. One small business, for example,
with fewer than 200 employees in 1977, spent more than £1.5m.
over the previous decade (at current prices) investing succ-
essively in two generations of polypropylene weaving equipment.

Not surprisingly, the upsurge of new investment spending in
the late 1960's was due to the need to equip for polypropylene.
McDowall, Draper and McGuinness give data at current prices
which show the changing emphasis from jute to polypropylene;
and while these, in the authors' view, considerably underestimate the level of investment in synthetics, they nonetheless
indicate the trend of investment by jute firms.

TABLE 4.31   Capital Investment in Jute and Synthetics (£'000)

	Jute	Synthetics
1968	1,648	
1969	742	
1970	438	435
1971	453	880
1972	330	725
1973	683	1,334
1974	474	1,509

Source: McDowall, S., P. Draper and T. McGuinness.   Trade
Adjustment and the British Jute Industry.
Unpublished Monograph, St.Andrews University, p.120.

RESEARCH AND DEVELOPMENT

Closely related to the question of investment in the industry
is the issue of research and development. The quality of the
former may be influenced by the extent of the latter. Prior
to 1946 there was no co-operative or group research carried
out in the Dundee jute industry; although reports suggest
that the largest firms in the industry had previously established their own individual laboratory facilities for research.
In 1946 however, under the auspices and with the financial
support of the Department of Scientific and Industrial
Research, the British Jute Trade Research Association was
formed. The Research Association was a purely voluntary body
(in contrast to such industries as wool and flax where joint
research was financed by a statutory levy), and was financed
by a subscription amounting to ½% of each firm's wage bill.
This sum raised by the industry was approximately matched by
the D.S.I.R. (later the Ministry of Technology). Some 97% of
jute spinners and manufacturers were members of the Association, and these were joined by merchants, brokers etc. as
well as by machinery manufacturers.

The Research Association carried out a number of activities.
These may be divided into three categories. First, long-term
basic research - covering work designed to discover and
examine the molecular basis of the physical and chemical
properties of jute. Second, short-term applied research and
development - whose purpose was to use research to solve
current problems, including the development of new markets
for jute products. Third, information, advisory and liaison
work - communicating the results of the previous categories
of work to firms, and the solving of day-to-day problems for
Association members.

Some idea of the scale of work carried out by the Association
can be gained from the data in Appendix Table 4.8 which covers
the period from its foundation until its winding up in its
earlier form and the creation of the Scottish Textile Research
Association in 1969.

During its period as a purely jute research association, the
B.J.T.R.A. appears to have carried out work of value to its
members. Some of its longer-term work never came to fruition.
It searched in vain for alternative sources of jute fibre for
Dundee, or indeed for alternative natural fibres similar to
jute. Likewise no dramatic breakthrough occurred in respect
of new end-use areas for jute. Some work was done on trying
to use jute in place of glass fibre in developing new resins;
but little came of this. Likewise there were few major advances in jute spinning and weaving machinery for which the
Association appears to have been responsible. The Association's achievements were perhaps more general. It undoubtedly
acted as a forum on technical matters for the industry. It
may also have had the effect of reducing the differences in
technical competence among the firms in the industry: bringing
more of the firms into line with the technologically more pro-
gressive. In this context it must be remembered that, given
the basis upon which the industry itself contributed to the
Association's finances, the research was overwhelmingly paid
for by the largest firms. One trade source estimated that
during the 1960's Sidlaw, Low & Bonar, and Scott & Robertson
were together contributing some 80% of the industry's total -
around 40% of the Association's total income.

With regard to jute itself, what the Association failed to do
was to find a replacement for the large-scale standard-product
markets such as sacking and linoleum backing which formed the
bulk of the industry's output in the immediate post-war period.
This, of course, may appear to be demanding much of the Association. What is relevant, however, is that as these markets
and that for tufted carpet backing disappeared in the latter
part of the 1960's, the jute industry and jute industry
research became less viable.

The coming of polypropylene brought about a reorientation of
the Association's work. By 1966 the Association had specifically decided that a proportion of its funds - around 30% -
should be spent on non-jute work - basically polyolefins
(B.J.T.R.A., 1966 Annual Report). The following year the
Association was able to report progress on its research on
polypropylene slit tape as an alternative to jute yarn. This
non-jute work was reported to account for over 20% of the

Association's research effort (B.J.T.R.A., 1967 Annual
Report); and its Reports indicate that the Association was
aware of the end-use market potential of polypropylene, and
also of the implications of such changes for jute.

Inevitably the Research Association decided eventually to
reflect its movement away from an undivided interest in jute
by a change of name. In 1969 the body became known as the
Scottish Textile Research Association. This body continued
in existence until 1975 when government matching of industry
support for research in this area came to an end. Some idea
of the extent of the Association's reorientation may be
gained from the following data relating to Government support.

TABLE 4.32 Research Association Government Grant

	"for Jute Work"	"for Polypropylene Work"
1966-7	£20,387	£7,964
1967-8	19,385	9,652
1968-9	15,726	18,310
1969-70	16,337	18,750
1970-1	10,942	25,302

Source: Trade and Industry, 23rd June 1971, p.618.

CONCLUSIONS

This chapter has been concerned with analysing the market
performance of the firms in what was at one time the Dundee
jute industry. This performance was specified in terms of
"financial" performance revealed through company accounting
data, labour productivity, investment and modernisation, and
research and development. It was emphasised that the
research based upon data relating to individual firms covered
only those businesses which were part of the jute industry in
1967, in respect of whom separate accounting data were
available, and which survived until 1977. The results of
tests on company accounting data are to be interpreted in
the light of the limitations imposed by such data, and also
on the basis of the assumptions regarding the manner in which
one interprets company accounting data discussed at the
beginning of the second section of this chapter.

Turning first to the data on company financial performance
analysed above, the first point to be made is that one's
findings broadly conform to the pattern of results of a
number of other cross-sectional and time-series studies
regarding performance across U.K. manufacturing industries.
This is so with regard to such relationships as that between

profitability and growth, size and growth, and size and
profitability. This is reassuring, for what it suggests is
that despite the smallness of sample size the results of the
tests can be accepted as not being totally abnormal.

Turning to the data on company financial performance, and
first to the results of the analysis of profitability, the
findings of our study were the absence of any trend of company profits relative to those for U.K. manufacturing industry
as a whole over the total period 1968-1977 (including intragroup profit variability), a remarkable stability of profit
performance between the two subperiods 1968-1972 and 1973-
1977 (including a significant maintenance of rank order among
the firms and a significant linear relationship between the
profit ratios in the two subperiods), and the usual relationship between profitability (as a dependent variable) and
average company size and growth (as measured by either assets
or sales) and with the two independent variables being incorporated jointly in the multiple linear regression. That
is, growth was a significant determinant but size was not.
These results, or the lack of significant difference from
expected behaviour, confirm some of our hypotheses and conclusions on the strategy of diversification dealt with in the
previous chapter. Not only did surviving firms in the
industry maintain their profitability relative to manufacturing industry over a period of quite dramatic change in their
traditional markets for jute; but despite individual firms
following quite different strategies from one another, the
rank order of their profit ratios in the two subperiods
remained high. Thus we might conclude that not only were the
surviving firms successful in surviving but that they even
held their ground relative to manufacturing industry as a
whole. Surprisingly too, despite following very different
survival strategies, the firms were successful in a very
homogeneous way, for example with regard to the lack of
change in intra-group profit variability over time and the
maintenance of rank order of company profitability between
the two subperiods. Thus our conclusion is that none of the
drama of the period so far as the collapse of traditional
markets is concerned worked its way through to company profitability.

In respect of corporate growth, the broad findings with
regard to our group of firms were that the rate of growth
over the period 1968-1977 (1969-77 with respect of employment)
was not significantly dependent upon opening size as measured
by either assets, sales or employment, that average profitability was, however, significantly linearly associated with
average growth. As in the case of profitability there was no

significant change in the growth rates of firms between the
two chosen subperiods. However, there was some disturbance
to the growth rank order between the two subperiods. Although
some of these findings were more significant with regard to
sales data compared with asset or employment figures, sales
data were regarded a priori as the most reasonable to use.
Although these findings are not surprising when taken in the
context of those of other econometric studies, they are
perhaps so with regard to our group of firms. One might have
expected, for example, that in our context large firms would
have had an advantage in growing (in a declining traditional
market) over smaller ones: that their size might have been
associated with greater financial weight, or management or
technical expertise (perhaps including a body of professional
managers separate from traditional owners) which would have
stimulated and facilitated a more effective strategy of response to Jute's decline compared with that of the small,
family owned businesses. That this has not been the case con-
firms again the conclusion in this respect in Chapter 3 on
diversification: that success in this area is not clearly
associated with identifiable variables such as company size.

With regard to labour productivity, Tables 4.18 - 4.20 suggest
at an aggregated level that the industry had some success in
this area in the 1950's, but that performance fell off badly
in the late 1960's and 1970's, although one can be far less
certain in interpreting recent statistics due to the problem
of allocating employees between jute and synthetics areas of
work. The data in Table 4.21 are more reliable and tell an
interesting story. The point to remember is that there was a
considerably greater reduction in female employment in the
industry compared with male employment during the main period
of adjustment. For example, in 1960 the jute industry
employed females and males in almost equal numbers. From that
date to 1977 the number of males employed declined by 40%
while the number of females fell by 68% to a point where
males comprised two-thirds of the work force.

Turning to the conclusions on labour productivity derived
from company accounting data (value added per employee) and
concerning relationships between this measure of labour
productivity and other company financial variables, it was
noted that size (as measured by assets and sales), growth and
capital intensiveness contributed strongly to increased labour
productivity when considered on a bivariate regression basis.
With regard to the growth of labour productivity, the results
were inconclusive so far as the impact of size and growth were
concerned. This applied also, rather surprisingly, in respect
of growth of capital intensiveness. These results are not in

conflict with those across U.K. manufacturing industry. At
the same time they do not reveal anything of special significance regarding our group's economic performance over this
period.

The data in respect of capital investment and modernisation in
the industry are of varying degrees of reliability. They do,
however, suggest that the industry responded to the potentially
more stable environment in the post 1948 period under Jute
Control by investing heavily in new plant and equipment.
Although it is not possible to offer a precise analyse of this
dimension of the industry's performance - for example by
relating this industry's new investment to its existing capital
stock or making such comparisons with U.K. manufacturing
industry as a whole - there does seem to be some impressionistic evidence to suggest that not only had the jute industry in
an absolute sense made considerable strides in modernising its
equipment over the period of the 1950's, but also that its
performance in this direction compared extremely favourably
with that of other textile industries. If the publication of
the 1948 Board of Trade Report gave an initial impetus to a
high level of investment in the industry, the effective operation of Jute Control and of the industry's trade pricing
agreements seem to have been sustaining forces. These,
certainly up to the early 1960's, allowed the jute industry to
believe that price competition from India and among home
producers would be limited. And while this study has elsewhere suggested that such price levels may have hastened the
entry and impact of polypropylene upon jute's end-use markets,
at the same time the investment must have provided for a higher
level of efficiency in jute spinning and manufacturing. Again,
imperfect though the data may be, figures suggest that, while
continuing to spend significant sums in maintaining its jute
plant in a modern state, the industry as a whole invested
heavily in synthetics plant and machinery from the late 1960's
onwards. This latter direction of spending was largely
responsible for the upsurge in total investment figures during
the late 1960's and early 1970's.

Finally, with respect to research and development, the industry's voluntary co-operative efforts in this area from 1946
onwards appear from discussions with those involved in this
aspect of the industry at the time to have had the effect of
improving the quality of product and production methods
across the industry. This was achieved by a pooling of resources for research and development in the industry, and by
spreading the results of such work more widely across the 97%
of spinners and manufacturers in the industry who were members
of the B.J.T.R.A. than would otherwise have been the case.

As in the area of capital investment expenditure, the industry appears to have responded quickly to the potential for developing polypropylene in terms of the switch of emphasis in its research and development expenditure.

This chapter has illustrated quantitatively a number of features of the traditional jute industry in a period of transition. Several characteristics stand out. First, there is evidence at a market level of a real effort by the industry to accomplish the transition. This is illustrated through the data on capital equipment expenditure and research and development effort. Second, the transition from almost complete dependence upon jute to a wider industrial textiles base and other interests was accomplished with quite remarkable smoothness by all of the surviving firms. This applied particularly to profitability, both relative to U.K. manufacturing industry, and with respect to profit performance within the group of firms and over subperiods within the years 1968-1977. Third, company size does not appear to have conferred overwhelming advantage on those firms within our group. Larger firms performed no better than smaller ones in respect of average profitability or growth over the period 1968-1977. These larger firms do, however, appear to have had an advantage in terms of the average level of labour productivity; and there is some evidence that the variability of their profits over time was lower than that of smaller competitors. These latter advantages did not however translate themselves into a better performance in the fundamental areas of profitability or growth.

Having summarised our findings and offered some analysis of these in the area of economic performance in this industry in the final section of this chapter, it remains in Chapter 5 to bring together all of the strands of findings and analysis in the study so far.

References

Allen, R.G.D. (1951). Statistics for Economists, 2nd ed. Hutchinson, London. p.14.

Amey, L.R. (1969). The Efficiency of Business Enterprises. Allen & Unwin, London. pp.1-21.

Bain, J.S. (1968). Industrial Organization, 2nd ed. Wiley, London. p.10.

Board of Trade (1948). Report of Jute Working Party. H.M.S.O., London.

Carter, C.F., and B.R. Williams (1957). Industry and Technical Progress. O.U.P., London.

Daniel, W.W., and J.C. Terrell (1975). Business Statistics: Basic Concepts and Methodology. Houghton Mifflin, Boston. pp.164-7.

Dundee Chamber of Commerce Journal. Chamber of Commerce, Dundee.

George, K.D. (1971). Industrial Organization. Allen & Unwin, London. p.25.

Howe, W.S. (1978). Industrial Economics. Macmillan, London.

L.R.4R.P. (1964). Incorporated Law Reporting Society, London. p.60.

Lenman, B. (1947). An Economic History of Modern Scotland. Batsford, London.

McDowall, S., P. Draper and T. McGuinnes. Trade Adjustment and the British Jute Industry. Unpublished Monograph, St. Andrews University. p.117.

Meeks, G. (1977). Disappointing Marriage: A Study of the Gains from Merger. C.U.P., Cambridge. p.2.

O'Brien, D.P., W.S. Howe, D.M. Wright and R.J. O'Brien (1979). Competition Policy, Profitability and Growth. Macmillan, London. pp. 7-11.

Pratten, C.F. (1971). Economies of Scale in Manufacturing Industry. C.U.P., Cambridge.

Robertson, L.F. (1962). Precognition to the Restrictive Practices Court. Dundee. p.112.

Siegel, S. (1958). Nonparametric Statistics for the Behavioral Sciences. McGraw-Hill Kogakusha, Tokyo.

Singh, A., and G. Whittington (1968). Growth, Profitability and Valuation. C.U.P., Cambridge.

Smyth, D.J., W.J. Boyes and D.E. Peseau (1975). Size, Growth, Profits and Executive Compensation in the Large Corporation. Macmillan, London.

Southgate, D.G. (1968). "Politics in Dundee". In S.J. Jones (Ed.), Dundee and District. British Association, Dundee. p.347

Times Publishing Co. (1952). Survey of the United Kingdom Jute Industry. London. p.24.

Walker, W.M. (1979). Juteopolis: Dundee and its Textile Workers 1885-1923. Scottish Academic Press, Edinburgh. pp.32-33.

Whittington, G. (1971). The Prediction of Profitability. C.U.P., Cambridge.

APPENDIX TABLE 4.1 Employment in the Jute Industry ('000)

	Males	Females	Total	Females: Males	Unemployment
1948	7.9	12.4	20.3	1.56:1	388
1949	7.2	10.0	17.2	1.39	1,361
1950	7.1	10.5	17.6	1.48	483
1951	7.7	11.1	18.8	1.44	291
1952	7.0	9.8	16.8	1.40	1,420
1953	8.1	11.8	19.9	1.46	619
1954	9.3	11.5	20.8	1.24	602
1955	8.8	11.0	19.8	1.25	1,087
1956	8.5	10.6	19.1	1.25	1,460
1957	8.6	10.1	18.7	1.17	1,646
1958	7.8	8.4	16.2	1.08	2,613
1959	8.2	8.7	16.9	1.06	1,258
1960	8.8	8.4	17.2	0.95	710
1961	8.3	8.6	16.9	1.04	1,655
1962	8.2	9.2	17.4	1.12	640
1963	8.6	8.4	17.0	0.98	945
1964	8.8	8.5	17.3	0.97	617
1965	8.9	8.6	17.5	0.97	459
1966	8.8	8.3	17.1	0.94	358
1967	8.0	7.3	15.3	0.91	950
1968	8.2	7.0	15.2	0.85	640
1969	8.5	6.9	15.4	0.81	542
1970	6.9	5.0	11.9	0.72	995
1971	6.1	4.2	10.3	0.69	1,415
1972	5.7	3.8	9.4	0.67	1,251
1973	5.5	3.5	9.0	0.64	931
1974	6.0	3.4	9.4	0.56	529
1975	5.3	2.8	8.1	0.53	730
1976	5.0	2.6	7.6	0.52	897
1977	5.3	2.7	8.0	0.51	923

Sources: Department of Employment (1971). British Labour
         Statistics - Historical Abstract 1886-1963.
         H.M.S.O., London; and subsequent annual editions
         of British Labour Statistics.

APPENDIX TABLE 4.2   Earnings and Hours Worked in Manufacturing
                                Industry*

	Men Aged 21 and Over		Women Aged 18 and Over	
	Average Weekly Earnings (£)	Average Weekly Hours Worked	Average Weekly Earnings (£)	Average Weekly Hours Worked
1948	7.17	46.5	3.74	41.6
1949	7.40	46.6	3.96	41.7
1950	7.83	47.5	4.16	42.1
1951	8.60	47.8	4.53	41.5
1952	9.24	47.7	4.84	41.8
1953	9.83	47.9	5.16	42.0
1954	10.61	48.5	5.45	42.0
1955	11.55	48.7	5.80	41.8
1956	12.11	48.2	6.00	41.5
1957	12.44	48.1	6.31	41.5
1958	13.06	47.6	6.58	41.2
1959	14.21	47.6	7.07	41.5
1960	15.16	47.4	7.41	40.4
1961	15.89	46.8	7.71	39.6
1962	16.34	46.2	8.03	39.3
1963	17.29	46.8	8.31	39.6
1964	18.67	46.9	8.94	39.3
1965	20.16	46.1	9.59	38.6
1966	20.78	45.0	10.06	38.0
1967	21.89	45.3	10.54	38.0
1968	23.62	45.8	11.31	38.2
1969	25.54	45.7	12.12	37.9
1970	28.91	44.9	13.98	37.7
1971	31.37	43.6	15.80	37.5
1972	36.20	44.1	18.34	37.7
1973	41.52	44.7	21.15	37.5
1974	49.12	44.0	27.05	37.2
1975	59.74	42.7	34.23	36.8
1976	67.83	43.5	40.71	37.2
1977	74.20	45.6	45.00	39.8

* Data are for manual workers in manufacturing industry.

Source: Department of Employment Gazette. H.M.S.O., London.

APPENDIX TABLE 4.3   Earnings and Hours Worked in Jute
                     Industry*

	Men Aged 21 and Over		Women Aged 18 and Over	
	Average Weekly Earnings (£)	Average Weekly Hours Worked	Average Weekly Earnings (£)	Average Weekly Hours Worked
1960	11.79	47.8	7.37	42.4
1961	11.93	45.6	7.54	40.8
1962	12.88	46.4	8.05	40.7
1963	13.43	46.0	8.13	40.5
1964	14.57	46.3	8.85	39.5
1965	15.71	47.0	9.21	39.6
1966	16.56	46.3	9.62	38.4
1967	18.08	45.6	10.36	38.3
1968	18.96	45.5	10.80	37.8
1969	21.47	45.2	12.32	37.7
1970	23.25	44.1	12.52	37.6
1971	25.02	44.9	15.70	38.0
1972	29.40	44.2	18.37	38.1
1973	33.14	43.3	21.72	37.5
1974	40.45	43.5	28.51	38.6
1975	50.50	42.8	34.74	36.1
1976	54.44	43.0	42.48	37.5
1977	56.36	42.7	42.47	36.3

* Figures are those for October each year

Sources: 1960-69 unpublished Department of Employment
         figures
         1970-   Department of Employment Gazette. H.M.S.O.,
                 London.

APPENDIX TABLE 4.4 Labour Productivity Comparisons

	Index of Raw Jute Consumption per Employee	Index of Output per Person Employed (Manuf. Industry)	3*	4**
	1950 = 100	1950 = 100		
1950	100	100		
1951	98	102		
1952	103	99		
1953	107	104		
1954	107	109		
1955	119	113		
1956	120	111		
1957	121	114		
1958	124	114		
1959	131	121		
1960	133	126		
1961	112	125		
1962	121	127		
1963	128	133	100	100
1964	122	144	95	106
1965	119	146	93	111
1966	116	149	91	114
1967	120	155	94	120
1968	118	166	92	140
1969	113	170	88	143
1970	118	172	92	148
1971	122	176	95	162
1972	133	187	104	173
1973	124	201	97	183
1974	102	198	80	172
1975	105	195	82	178
1976	101	203	79	191
1977	94	202	73	201

 * as in col. 1 1963 = 100
** as in col. 2 for Textiles 1963 = 100

Sources: Table 4.20, and British Labour Statistics. H.M.S.O.,
         London.

APPENDIX TABLE 4.5   Capital Investment (£'000)

	Cumulative Total	Annual	Price Index*	Annual at 1970 Prices	3-Year Moving Average
1945	500	500	..	..	
1946	1,000	500	..	..	
1947	1,500	500	..	..	
1948	2,000	500	40.3	1,240	
1949	2,500	500	41.2	1,214	1,212
1950	3,000	500	42.3	1,182	1,529
1951	4,000	1,000	45.7	2,190	1,677
1952	4,850	850	51.2	1,660	1,897
1953	5,830	980	53.2	1,840	2,097
1954	7,330	1,500	53.7	2,790	2,133
1955	8,330	1,000	56.6	1,770	2,346
1956	9,830	1,500	60.5	2,480	1,983
1957	10,920	1,090	63.9	1,700	1,773
1958	11,670	750	65.8	1,140	1,177
1959	12,130	460	66.5	690	817
1960	12,600	420	67.5	620	627
1961	13,000	400	70.2	570	630
1962	13,500	500	71.7	700	653
1963	14,000	500	73.0	690	907
1964	15,000	1,000	75.0	1,330	1,143
1965	16,100	1,100	77.9	1,410	1,390
1966	17,250	1,150	80.3	1,430	1,397
1967	18,350	1,100	81.3	1,350	1,577
1968	20,000	1,650	84.7	1,950	1,550
1969	21,250	1,250	90.8	1,350	1,850
1970	24,500	2,250	100.0	2,250	1,953
1971	27,000	2,500	110.7	2,260	2,347
1972	30,000	3,000	118.8	2,530	2,623
1973	34,000	4,000	130.0	3,080	2,863
1974	38,500	4,500	150.9	2,980	2,560
1975	41,500	3,000	185.5	1,620	1,667
1976	42,500	1,000	247.3	400	732
1977	43,000	500	282.0	177	

* From C.S.O., Price Index Numbers for Current Cost
  Accounting. H.M.S.O., London.

Sources: Trade Statistics.

Appendix Table 4.6

Capital Investment 1945-1977 : Cumulative Total (current
                                                    prices)

Source : Appendix Table 4.5

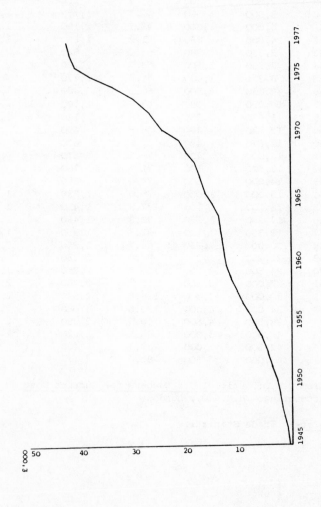

Appendix Table 4.7

Annual Capital Investment 1948-1977 at 1970 Prices

Source : Appendix Table 4.5

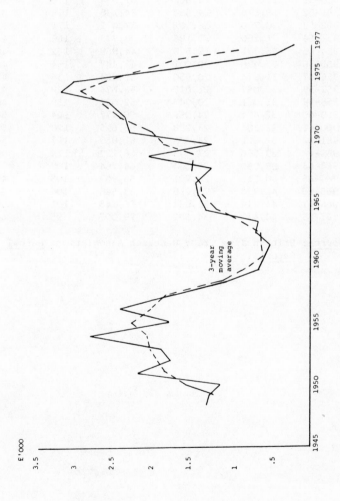

APPENDIX TABLE 4.8 British Jute Trade Research Association

| | Income | | Total | Member-ship | Employ-ees |
	Industry	Government			
1946-47	..	..	£18,502	138	4
1947-48	£13,463	£10,557	24,020	160	12
1948-49	15,523	13,001	28,524	170	22
1949-50	16,963	14,346	31,309	172	29
1950-51	17,372	14,662	32,034	176	30
1951-52	19,579	14,559	34,138	175	36
1952-53	20,770	16,301	37,071	171	39
1953-54	21,580	17,193	38,773	166	43
1954-55	25,331	19,538	44,869	152	48
1955-56	27,496	20,001	47,497	154	43
1956-57	31,874	20,950	52,824	136	45
1957-58	32,057	21,617	53,674	129	45
1958-59	31,081	20,943	52,024	139	46
1959-60	32,425	24,052	56,477	124	50
1960-61	33,387	23,228	56,615	120	50
1961-62	37,621	24,238	61,859	117	50
1962-63	39,596	27,533	66,129	114	50
1963-64	38,960	25,604	64,764	108	50
1964-65	40,116	26,791	66,907	105	40
1965-66	41,330	28,218	69,548	104	43
1966-67	44,314	31,831	76,145	101	39
1967-68	44,415	34,592	79,007	95	44

Source: British Jute Trade Research Association, Annual
        Reports.

APPENDIX TABLE 4.9   Linear Regression of Firm Size and
                     Vertical Integration

Dependent variable: 10-year average ratio of value added to
                    sales

Size Measure	Constant	b	t	R^2	Rho	DW
Average assets	0.334	-0.00001	5.0000**	0.3742	-0.4214	1.3346
Opening assets	0.335	-0.00001	2.5000**	0.3766	-0.3769	1.2518
Average sales	0.338	-0.000003	3.0000***	0.4196	-0.4679*	1.4121
Opening sales	0.338	-0.000006	3.0000***	0.4134	-0.5393**	1.2931
Average employ.	0.338	-0.00003	3.0000***	0.2235	-0.4647*	1.2419
Opening employ.	0.336	-0.00003	1.5000	0.2361	-0.4665*	1.2873

Growth Measure						
Assets	0.313	-0.00027	0.1125	0.0010	-0.0947	1.1786
Sales	0.313	0.00013	0.0361	0.0001	0.0393	1.1920
Employment	0.313	-0.00004	0.0108	0.0000	-0.0054	1.1836

Significance levels: *10%, **5%, ***1%, ****0.1%

DW: all of the statistics were within the indeterminate range
    except that relating to vertical integration and average
    sales where the statistic was not significant at 10%.

CHAPTER 5

CONCLUSIONS

INTRODUCTION

Jack Downie (1958) justified his meagre one and a half pages
of conclusions at the end of his book The Competitive Process
by a reference to Keynes' famous remark on economics being an
"apparatus of the mind", and a suggestion that "it is because
economics is as he (Keynes) described it that few books on
economic subjects have a very lengthy chapter on conclusions".
It nonetheless seems both appropriate and possible to draw a
number of conclusions from this study, and these relate both
to the behaviour of firms in an individual market and to the
broader topic of resource allocation and efficiency in
general. Indeed there appears to be a growing realisation
and confidence that studies of individual firms or industries
can lead on to the formulation of useful generalisations on
economic behaviour; and also that the study of firm or individual-industry decision making at the microeconomic level can
throw light upon questions of the overall or macro-economic
operation of the economy. Furthermore this relationship
between microeconomic and macroeconomic performance may be
particularly significant in the area of economic growth where
a major determinant of the rate of expansion of firms and of
an economy is the rate at which new technologies are developed
or adopted. This particular study, being one largely concerned with an environment of technological change and of the
process of the adaptation to new technology, is one in which
it should be especially possible to highlight certain wider
implications on the basis of observation of a single industry.

This study has been one of a declining industry, indeed of an
industry demand for whose traditional products for sacking and
bags and for yarn and cloth for the carpet industry collapsed

very rapidly over a relatively short period of time at the
end of the 1960's. To give one example in respect of a major
end use, jute's share of the market for the primary backing
of tufted carpets fell from more than 90% in 1967 to less than
5% in 1974. In such an environment a number of questions and
issues automatically arise. First, was the traditional jute
industry in any sense responsible for its own demise, or for
the timing or pace of its downfall? Was it the case, for
example, that arrangements of one form or another among firms
in the jute industry, or simply the general uncompetitiveness
of the traditional market, caused new products to take over
from jute on a price or quality basis? If such a takeover was
in some sense inevitable, was the process speeded up by conduct on the part of jute manufacturers? Second, were changes
in demand for jute or in the accompanying technology foreseen
by firms in the traditional market? How aware were the original jute manufacturers of the possibility of technical obsolescence in respect of jute yarn and cloth; and what steps were
being taken to deal with the situation? For example, were any
of the jute manufacturers responsible for major developments
in polypropylene? Third, what was the reaction of the original jute manufacturers to the commercial development of polypropylene from the mid 1960's onwards? Fourth, and related to
the previous question, how far did the traditional jute manufacturing firms participate in new technology as it related
either to jute or to polypropylene? It is in an attempt to
answer some of these questions that these Conclusions are
written.

CHANGES IN MARKETS AND MARKET STRUCTURE

As mentioned in the Introduction to this chapter, our study
has been one of market decline so far as the traditional jute
industry is concerned. This decline came from two sources:
radical change in technology (from handling and transporting
goods in jute bags to bulk handling and containerisation),
and substitution of synthetic fibres (predominantly polypropylene) for jute. To the question, could jute in the long term
have competed more effectively against these new methods, the
answer must be no. There is no indication that other than
dramatically lower jute prices could have preserved a container
end-use market for jute, or that polypropylene's inroads into
jute's traditional markets were not the result predominantly
of better technological performance combined with lower prices
given the nature of the synthetic raw material. It was,
however, noted in Chapter 2 that the system of Jute Control
and the restrictive trading agreements did have the effect of
artificially raising the price of jute above world levels.

Control, for example, "marked up" the price of some imports
of jute goods by up to 50%; and in other areas there was a
complete ban on imports from Calcutta - Dundee prices in some
cases being up to 75% above those of potential imports
(McDowall and Draper, 1978). Furthermore, attention has been
drawn to the fact that quite apart from the impact of Control,
jute manufacturers in the U.K. do not appear in the late
1960's and early 1970's to have been prepared to fight any
rearguard action along the price dimension of competition to
maintain the position of jute in its existing markets.

The history of changing markets for firms in the traditional
jute industry is that of the disappearance of former jute end
uses, and of the efforts by most firms to participate in the
necessary technological change to avoid total loss of
business. Thus although, as was noted in Chapter 3, there are
one or two small spinners who have remained entirely in jute,
satisfying demand largely for woven carpet yarns, and although
many of the large firms still combine jute spinning and
weaving with synthetic interests, most firms have moved significantly into polypropylene or other man-made fibres, or into
more diversified interests. The result of changes in technology is that although the carpet industry is now responsible
for purchasing a much greater share of total jute output - the
proportion having risen from around 50% in the late 1950's to
80% by the early 1970's - it can give the jute industry only a
fraction of the custom which it once did.

The main point about changes in markets brought about by the
growing significance of polypropylene is that the former jute
manufacturers are now operating in a much more sophisticated
market. Instead of buying on a world market having some of
the characteristics of perfect competition on the raw material
supply side, the synthetics weavers or extruders are now purchasing their input requirements from the large constituents
of the petroleum and chemical oligopolies. These are producing propylene as a by-product of refining crude oil (or
natural gas liquids in the case of the United States), the
propylene emerging along with ethylene from the by-product
naphtha. The attitude towards the production and pricing of
these products by the major oil companies is therefore of
considerable importance to the Dundee industry. Nor should
it be forgotten that although some 65% of polypropylene
textile output is processed in Dundee and the surrounding
area, a major competitor to these local firms exists in the
form of Pachogue Plymouth, the AMOCO subsidiary. This
business is a fully integrated concern, being part of Standard
Oil of Indiana. So far as sales of polypropylene output are
concerned, it has to be remembered that textile uses are

largely (70%) dependent upon the tufted carpet industry,
characterised by cyclical trading conditions and concentrated
buying power. Thus, although polypropylene has a wide variety
of uses in various forms, the local Dundee industry is heavily
oriented towards carpet backing and packaging end uses, about
70% of output going into the former and a further 8% into the
latter.

One of the questions posed in the introduction to this chapter
related to the degree to which the industry as a whole, and
individual constituent firms, had recognised the need for
change away from dependence upon jute to the new market areas,
and had responded to the need. At an individual level there
is no doubt that a number of firms responded quickly to the
possibilities of textile applications of polypropylene. As
early as 1965 Low & Bonar and Sidlaw each acquired a 40%
interest in Polytape Ltd., a subsidiary of British Ropes (now
Bridon) which had been established to explore the possibility
of producing tape yarns from extruded polypropylene film.
These two local firms went on to establish their own tape
weaving subsidiary Synthetic Fabrics (Scotland). Other firms
which invested in some aspects of polypropylene technology at
an early date were Don Bros. Buist, Caird, and Scott & Fyfe -
the latter two being relatively small firms. Other businesses
were more reluctant to enter the polypropylene market at an
early stage; and some of course followed other lines of
diversification. At first there may have been some doubt as
to how far and how rapidly polypropylene would displace jute
in the latter's established end-use areas; and this feature
no doubt discouraged some firms from following the example of
those mentioned above. Indeed generally there seems to have
been a lack of appreciation as to just how quickly jute was
likely to be superseded by polypropylene. Thus at the end of
1968 one trade source (Dundee Chamber, Sept. 1968, p.206) was
of the opinion that "for the primary backing of tufted
carpets ... polypropylene is seen not so much as a fibre that
will make inroads into jute but as an additional fibre" - yet
jute was almost entirely eliminated from this market by the
early 1970's. Again even at the end of 1971, and instancing
in particular the use of jute in woven carpets, the same
source (Dundee Chamber, Dec.1971, p.640) felt that "there are
still large markets for which jute is technically better, and
does a superior job than any known man-made fibre" - although
this market too is now increasingly catered for by polypropylene. Thus one can say that although a number of firms in
the industry took an early part in the new technology, the
pace at which polypropylene was to displace jute was probably
underestimated by the trade as a whole.

Another relevant characteristic in this context is the relationship between the rate at which firms in the industry moved
into new market areas or adopted new technologies, and
variables such as company size and existing commitment to the
jute industry. Very few clear relationships have emerged from
the research. As indicated in Chapter 3 (Tables 3.7 - 3.13)
there was no clear statistical relationship revealed by the
parametric statistical tests, although opening size (by sales)
was significantly greater for diversified than non-diversified
firms in terms of the nonparametric tests which constitute
more robust evidence with regard to our group of firms.
Again in Chapter 4, as an indirect measure of the adoption of
new technologies and markets, no evidence was found (Tables
4.11, 4.15 and 4.18) of any parametric or nonparametric relationship between opening firm size and growth. This evidence
certainly does not suggest that large firms had any enormous
technical, financial or managerial advantage over their
smaller competitors in adapting to new market conditions.
Thus while some of the smaller spinning firms have continued
to remain entirely in the jute industry - preferring not to
have to face the problem of learning new technologies and
raising additional capital - others in this size category
were among the earliest to invest in the new technology. Likewise, while some large firms have successfully diversified and
adopted new technologies, this has by no means been the case
with all.

Regarding the relationship between diversification and extent
of existing commitment to the traditional jute industry, it is
worth noting that Low & Bonar - which although a large firm
never occupied a predominant place in the jute industry - has
consistently been a diversifier, while Sidlaw - which has
traditionally been the market leader in jute - has proved to
be less committed to synthetics and not uniformly successful
in other diversified areas. The more conservative reaction
of Sidlaw with respect to jute is perhaps best summed up by a
reported comment by its chairman in 1968: "I'd still rather
be in jute 100 per cent. than in synthetics 100 per cent."
(Financial Times 18.10.68).

A part of the material in the two previous paragraphs can be
illuminated by reference to the concept of barriers to exit.
In our case one has to mind barriers not only to the exit of
firms in a total sense but also to the transfer of firms into
new technologies quite evidently superseding their existing
methods of serving particular markets. There is evidence of
both of these phenomena in the jute industry. We saw in the
third section of Chapter 2 that a number of company deaths
only occurred finally after many years of financial losses;

and the reluctant attitude of some firms as regards leaving their dependence upon jute to invest in polypropylene has been referred to immediately above. It is interesting that at least one survey of the phenomenon of barriers to exit (Caves and Porter, 1976), while referring to the "technical" causes of these such as durable and specific capital assets, specific qualities of a labour force (and the cost of redundancy payments), and regional concentration of producers, also gives considerable emphasis to "the importance of intangible and managerial exit barriers relative to those linked to tangible assets". This relative emphasis receives support from our study of the jute industry. Obviously the industry in the 1960's was characterised by the existence of plant and machinery which was highly durable and specific, and some of which was so old that from the point of view of some accountants its use entailed no charge against the profits of the business. The industry's labour force too was regarded by some as being rather specific and not necessarily adaptable to having to cope with new synthetic fibre technologies. The geographical concentration of the jute industry around Dundee may also have inhibited thinking in terms of any dramatic geographical shift of firm's activities. Nonetheless the different speeds at which various firms reacted to the decline of the traditional jute market, and differences in the rapidity with which they adopted new technologies both lend weight to the emphasis of Caves and Porter upon managerial factors in this area.

Turning now to the changes in the general market environment, it would appear on the face of it that the operation of Jute Control and of the restrictive trading agreements must have protected the Dundee industry from both foreign and domestic competition, and therefore in some sense led to a misallocation of resources. Indeed it was the explicit purpose of these arrangements to protect the local industry. A system such as Control, which in 1962 had the effect of creating an absolute import barrier in respect of 80% of total U.K. jute goods production, could not have had any other effect than to permit the survival of firms which would otherwise have gone out of business. Indeed one study (McDowall, Draper and McGuinness, 1976) suggests that in the late 1950's and early 1960's the abandonment of Control's import protection would have led to the "virtual extinction" of the Dundee industry. It is difficult to be more precise regarding the impact of Control upon the size of the industry. There were no major exits from the market up to the later 1960's except for five disappearances in 1959, and these did not coincide with changes in Control regulations. This does not, however, mean that the earlier withdrawal of import protection would not have resulted in a

much faster slimming down of the Dundee industry. The major
adjustment to Control in 1963 and 1964 was not, correspondingly, accompanied by any apparent reduction in the number of
firms in the market. Indeed the industry itself did not
appear to expect the change to have a dramatic effect (Dundee
Chamber, Dec. 1964, p.241). The point about any analysis of
the impact of the relaxation and ending of Control is that
many other variables were changing at the same time. In
particular, the ending of the industry's restrictive trading
agreements early in 1963 coincided with a further reduction
in tariff restrictions; and the final ending of Control's
functions in 1969 and its replacement with a purely quota
system of import limitation took place just at the time when
polypropylene was beginning to make serious inroads into
jute's hold on the tufted carpet backing market. Most comm-
entators would thus agree that Control moved from a position
in the 1950's where it was indispensable to the survival of
the Dundee industry to one in the later 1960's where technological change had made it irrelevant.

McDowall, Draper and McGuinness have pointed to a more intri-
cate relationship between Control and technological change.
The price levels for jute in the U.K. established by Control
not only gave domestic producers a cushion with which to
finance modernisation and ultimately diversification into
synthetics spinning and weaving (including predominantly polypropylene), but also hastened the adoption by carpet manufacturers in this country of polypropylene in place of jute
because of the enhanced price differential compared with,
say, the situation in the United States. Certainly those in
the industry today with whom the matter was discussed concede
that the price levels established under Control were fair,
and possibly even generous. They admit that such price
levels allowed small marginal firms to remain in the market,
and accept that there was a wide spread of productive efficiency among manufacturers. However, one can at the same time
point to considerable investment in modernised plant over the
decades following 1945, and also, as detailed in Chapter 4,
to increased labour productivity. Furthermore the number
of independent businesses in the local industry did fall by
23% from 1945 to 1967, indicating that the various arrangements did not guarantee complete survival for all of the
firms in the market; and at the very least one can say that
no few firms entered the market - although textile firms outside Dundee probably considered that they faced considerable
barriers to entry through failure to enjoy external economies
of scale comparable to Dundee producers in contemplating expansion into the jute market.

Control, therefore, appears to have given the Dundee producers
a temporary protection from inevitable decline. Any loss of
welfare along the lines of traditional resource misallocation
here appears to have been the price paid for a temporary maintenance of employment in a city dominated by a single declining industry. It might also be possible to argue that the
temporary respite from traditional overseas competition
granted by Control did more adequately equip the industry to
meet the later technological (Schumpeterian) competition.
One must, however, at the same time recognise that not only
do such arrangements as Control deny domestic consumers
access to cheaper goods from overseas (and also artificially
deny overseas exporters the opportunity to compete on equal
terms with U.K. producers), but also that total consumption
of such protected goods is reduced to a level below what it
would otherwise have been without protection. This effect, it
was suggested, in the jute industry probably eventually led to
an increase in the rate at which jute was superseded by polypropylene in major end uses. Furthermore, subsidies to a
particular geographically concentrated industry, such as jute,
merely protect that industry and encourage it to maintain its
hold on its existing labour force, rather than encourage new
industries to take up employment in the area. Finally, of
course, if a protected industry is not totally concentrated
geographically, then firms and employees in this market are
protected by tariffs regardless of the total economic conditions of the region in which they are located. It is against
these potential sources of resource misallocation that one has
to set the benefits for the industry or local employment
claimed to arise from tariff or other trade restrictions (see
Corden and Fels, 1976).

The comments above apply with equal force to any analysis of
the impact upon the industry of the trading agreements. The
anticompetitive effect of these was continued beyond 1963 by
the operation of an information agreement and the practice of
price leadership - for both of which the industry was indebted
to Sidlaw. Both of these arrangements were, however, brought
to an end by the mid 1960's, and the impact of this ending is
difficult to distinguish from the termination of Control and
the emergence of polypropylene. Undoubtedly the trading
agreements had, together with the geographical concentration
of the industry, created an environment within the market
which discouraged rivalry in general. It is unlikely in this
context that firms minimised costs or eagerly sought to increase sales through price competition. Such an arrangement
could not, however, survive the impact of an entirely new
product in respect of which there were non-Dundee competitors,
whose technology was new and again originated outwith Dundee,

and in respect of which there was considerable international
competition.

Again with regard to the price leadership which emerged in
the industry following the ending of the trade pricing agreements, this practice does not seem to have survived the impact
of polypropylene's entry into traditional jute end-use areas.
It is possible that Sidlaw continued to exert some form of
nominal leadership of the "barometric" type in the industry by
virtue of its size and its earlier role in the Jute Information Bureau. However, the very rapid adoption of polypropylene
in the tufted carpet backing market at the end of the 1960's,
and the continued loss of market share of woven carpets in
favour of tufteds (woven carpet manufacturers' sales fell from
28.9 m.sq.m. in 1967 to 25.4 m.sq.m. in 1975, representing a
decline in total carpet market share by volume from 32.4% to
15.8% over the period) created market pressures which no
desire to maintain prices could overcome. From the late 1960's
onwards there is evidence (Craiks, 1967 Annual Report) of
"serious and widespread ... price cutting" having occurred,
and this continued into the 1970's with the observation by
another company chairman (Buist Spinning Co., 1977 Annual
Report) of how "when supply exceeds demand some spinners introduce cut prices and thus set a lower level of profitability".
This suggests that as with other potentially anti-competitive
structure or conduct characteristics of this market, the rapid
contraction of the traditional market was sufficient to nullify
any real impact of these.

Given that this study has been one of market decline - and in
the period 1967-1977 jute cloth output fell by 79% and yarn
output by 59% - it is not surprising that a major feature of
market structure has been a sharp reduction in the number of
firms. As Table 2.1 in Chapter 2 indicates, the number of
firms fell by 50% over a decade: from 30 in 1967 to 15 in
1976. Some part of this reduction is accounted for by surviving firms such as Low & Bonar, and Caird (Dundee) ceasing to
be A.J.S.M. members (our definition of firms in the industry),
although this in itself is a fair reflection of their exit
from the traditional jute market. The major part of the reduction in numbers over this period however - 12 out of 15 -
is due partially to acquisition and largely to the total demise of smaller firms. Of the 12 disappearances, 7 definitely
fell into the latter category; and this fate was particularly
characteristic of non-integrated weaving concerns, such as
R.G. Kennedy, T.L. Miller, and Don & Duncan. Neither these
disappearances nor the mergers which took place appear on the
face of things to raise any major resource-allocation
problems, although the author did receive a written communi-

cation from a senior director of one firm stating that from
1970 onwards his firm had followed an explicit policy of
"under the counter rationalisation" in terms of acquiring and
subsequently closing down jute manufacturing facilities of its
competitors. Nonetheless, on the whole the businesses which
left the industry at this time were predominantly small and
family owned/managed. Furthermore, some of the mergers or
acquisitions, such as J.D. Wilkie's taking over of fellow
Kirriemuir producer Ogilvie Brothers in 1971, or the earlier
more significant merger which created Scott & Robertson,
meant improved viability for the firms concerned, and possibly
increased competition for the existing large firms in the
market. On the other hand some apparent acquisitions, such as
Halley's takeover of Spalding & Valentine, or Low & Bonar's
acquisition of Wm. Ferguson, were in fact contractions of the
traditional industry as the jute operations of the two victims
were rapidly closed down. It is interesting, indeed, to note
that in only two cases - those of Sidlaw's acquisitions of
Duke & Lowson and the Tayport Spinning Co., and Don Bros.
Buist's purchase of J. & J. Smart - did major producers in the
industry take over and continue in operation additional facilities. In general, therefore, the industry's contraction went
ahead in a gradual and "civilised" manner: the only point to
notice being that had the smaller family businesses not gone
out of existence, then Sidlaw and Scott & Robertson and the
remaining larger firms might have found their own continuance
in the industry more difficult.

It is impossible to conclude firmly whether those enterprises
which did go out of business were the least efficient. Did
the decline of the industry (for we have seen that any tendency to more aggressive competition among the firms was earlier
kept in check by the operation of Control and the trading
agreements) have the effect of eliminating the less efficient
firms before the more efficient? In the absence of company
accounting data the answer must be inconclusive. Possibly
more important causes of demise appear to have been the size
and position within the industry structure (including the
extent of integration) on the part of the firms. Because the
weaving side of the traditional jute industry declined so
much more rapidly than the spinning side (the former by 79%
in the decade to 1977 in volume terms compared with 59% in
respect of the latter), those firms which were solely weavers
were at a particular disadvantage compared with those which
also had spinning capacity. The fairly rapid disappearance
of the pure weavers at the end of the 1960's also gave the
integrated spinners and weavers additional work for their
looms at a time when the amount of weaving work was diminishing. As regards the effect of firm size, deaths were much

more common among small than large firms; and it may be sur-
mised that in addition to the forces mentioned above, the
necessary change to an unfamiliar, capital intensive technology was much less attractive, even where it was possible, for
such firms compared with their larger counterparts.

PRODUCTIVITY AND INVESTMENT

Since these two phenomena have a close relationship, it would
appear to be sensible to discuss them together in assessing
market performance. As usual, the indices for measuring the
variables were not perfect for our purpose; but the general
conclusion in the former area is that significant improvements in labour productivity were made by the industry.
Rather surprisingly, however, in the light of further comments
below, the industry does not compare favourably with roughly
similar markets in this performance dimension. The following
data (which relate to volume changes) are from a fairly recent
cross-sectional study of labour productivity.

TABLE 5.1 Annual Average Compound Rates of Growth

	1954-1963		1963-1973	
	Gross Output	Outper per Operative	Gross Output	Output per Operative
Jute	-1.0	1.4	-3.0	2.9
Spinning and Doubling	-3.7	3.3	-1.0	4.3
Weaving	-3.0	4.3	-1.9	4.4
Woollen and Worsted	0.6	2.8	-1.1	3.9
81 Manufacturing Industries Average	2.5	2.9	3.2	4.3

Source: Wragg, R. and J. Robertson (1978), "Britain's
        Industrial Performance since the War", Department
        of Employment Gazette, May 1978, pp.513-15.

It would seem, therefore, that comparing the jute industry's
labour productivity with that of other industries of similar
technology and comparable experience of market contraction,
and with manufacturing industry as a whole, the performance
along this dimension has not been totally satisfactory. It
may be claimed that labour productivity in jute is understated if some part of a factory workforce is weaving polypropylene or spinning nylon staple while the whole of the
employment of the establishment is regarded as falling into
the "jute" category. However, similar problems are likely
in the case of the Spinning and Doubling or Weaving categories above due to the movement from cotton spinning and

weaving to, for example, spinning of nylon staple or weaving
of rayon. It is, of course, difficult to know what sort of
impact such imperfections have on statistical comparisons.
Our only conclusion must be that although improvements in
labour productivity seem by themselves to have been reasonable, a still better performance has been achieved in other
comparable markets.

With regard to new investment, data was constructed on the
basis of comments from a number of sources. The result is
Appendix Table 4.5 in Chapter 4. Again the actual data confirm the pattern of the history of the industry. There was
significant re-equipment in the immediate post-war period up
to the late 1950's, followed by a lull which in turn preceded
the investment boom of the late 1960's and early 1970's associated with polypropylene extrusion and weaving. Qualitative
assessment of this investment is difficult. It is, however,
noticeable that with regard to the most recent round of
capital expenditure that the equipment and new developments
in this area have come from abroad. Innovation has come not
from the traditional home of textile machinery manufacture in
this country but from overseas: from Switzerland (Sulzer),
Germany (Dornier), and from Italy (Smit). The local textile
industry itself, however, appears to have been forward in
keeping its machinery up-to-date, and in this respect presents
a very different picture to that painted by Caroline Miles
(1968, p.19) of the Lancashire textile industry.

> "A characteristic feature of the British cotton
> industry over the last fifty years, perhaps
> even longer, has been its lack of interest in
> technological development and (in) the use of
> new production methods and equipment."

The comparison with cotton is an interesting and valid one so
far as jute is concerned. Both industries have experienced
distinct secular decline over the past decades; in both cases
the technology of the traditional industry is relatively
static while capable of continuous improvement; and again both
industries, following Government inquiry, have received some
form of special support. The contrast between Miles' picture
of cotton and our own view of the jute industry is thus to
the credit of the latter. The remaining interesting feature
of the jute industry in this context is the way in which
investment and asset growth has not been the prerogative of
larger firms; and it is obviously heartening from the point
of view of the local economy to find low barriers to such
growth in the industry.

ACCOUNTING OR FINANCIAL MARKET PERFORMANCE

Throughout the second section of Chapter 4 it was pointed out
that the findings on the financial or accounting performance
of our firms were not out of line with those of U.K.-wide
cross-sectional and time-series analysis of company performance. Because of this lack of conflict, the purpose of this
section is to interpret and offer conclusions on the statistical findings as they relate to our particular market only.

With regard to profit ratios, the failure to detect any trend
over the period 1968-1977, either in respect of unadjusted or
relative ("real") profitability, or with regard to intragroup
profit variability, is surprising. It will be remembered also
that subperiod analysis of profitability performance (using
subperiods 1968-1972 and 1973-1977) failed to reveal any
"disturbance" in this dimension of market performance. Even
allowing for the fact that the data used cover the performance
of 16 continuing firms, and therefore ignore that of firms
which failed to survive the period of transition, they do give
one a reasonable picture of the industry over a major period
of adjustment. It should also be remembered that the market
performance of the 16 continuing firms to which our data apply
represents the outcome of a variety of strategies in the
market, including the course total abandonment of the jute
industry in any form by a number of the companies. The profitability and other data thus refer both to continuing jute
firms and to those which within the period left the industry.

The absence of any trend in the level or group variability of
profits, even in respect of a group of surviving firms in a
declining market, is surprising. What it suggests is that
there was no financial penalty as a result of the process of
transition; that no one firm made a particularly better or
worse job of managing the process of change than any other,
and that the (surviving) firms in general managed the process
of adjustment quite well. These conclusions are supported by
the absence of any relationship between firm size and profitability over the period reported in Tables 4.6 and 4.9. The
data in Tables 4.8 and 4.9 emphasise the existence in this
particular market of the usual relationship at the firm level
between size and the time variability of profits.

The normal or expected relationships between growth and such
independent variables as size and profitability were
established in Tables 4.11 to 4.15 and 4.18 of Chapter 4. As
emphasised in that chapter, what is significant is that
growth in this case may be taken as a prime index of relative
survival ability and competence in dealing with change. It

is clear that size has been of no assistance here. This
indicates either that economic scale is of no value or significance in growing, or that "managerial" factors have swamped
any relationship which might have existed between growth and
size, with smaller firms having some inbuilt advantage in
responding to change. Contrary to the case of profit performance there appears to have been some disruption to growth
patterns breaking the experience of the firms into the two
subperiods 1968-1972 and 1973-1977.

COMPARISON WITH OTHER DECLINING INDUSTRIES

It would seem appropriate to make some brief comparison of
the performance of the Dundee jute trade with at least one
other declining textile industry in order to note any particular contrasting or parallel conduct or performance. Two
obvious industries which could have been used are the Lancashire cotton industry and the Yorkshire woollen trade. Both,
as their names imply, are highly localised. The former of
these was chosen for individual comparison on the grounds of
having more in common with the jute industry; and while no
claim is made for a depth of knowledge of this industry such
as has been accumulated in respect of jute, sufficient study
has been carried out to make relevant comparisons.

As in the case of jute, the Lancashire cotton textile
industry has gone through a period of considerable decline
this century, as the data below indicate.

TABLE 5.2 Output of U.K. Cotton Textile Industry

	Yarn '000 tonnes	Woven Cloth M. lin. metres
1946	299.8	1,486
1953	314.0	1,704
1956	270.7	1,453
1963	178.8	927
1970	125.8	627
1977	84.4	368

Source : Annual Abstract of Statistics. H.M.S.O., London.

In 1914 Lancashire had 40% of world textile capacity, and
accounted for 60% of international trade in cotton. The
industry in 1912 employed directly around 750,000 people, and
was responsible for a quarter by value of U.K. exports
(Tippett, 1969). After a temporary post-war boom, which came
to an end in 1921, demand slumped as Indian and Japanese
markets fell to domestic producers who also ate into some of

Lancashire's other export markets. (Prior to World War I
some 85% of Lancashire output was exported.) Output of cotton
cloth in 1937 at 4,000m. yards was exactly half the corresponding figure for 1912. Rationalisation in the industry occurred
as a result of the mergers over this period (the formation of
the Lancashire Cotton Corporation under the auspices of the
Bank of England in 1929 brought around 15% of spinning capacity
into the hands of a single firm, and Combined English Mills was
formed in the same year), and of the operation of the Spindles
Board established under the 1936 Cotton Spinning Industry Act.
The Board, financed by a levy on the industry, paid spinners
and weavers to scrap capacity; and by 1937 the industry had
reduced its 1912 capacity by about one third, although output,
as noted above, had halved over the period.

As in the case of jute, the cotton industry was "concentrated"
during World War II. Again as in the case of jute, a Cotton
Control was established; and, operating from 1947 as the Raw
Cotton Commission, was the sole agency for importing and distri-
buting raw cotton until the trade was returned to private
hands in 1954. Demand for cotton goods was buoyant immediately
after 1945; and indeed labour shortages were a problem. The
industry's inefficiency and poor long-term prospects were,
however, recognised, and a number of reports on the industry
was published, including one in 1946 by a Board of Trade Cotton
Working Party. This did not, however, recommend a system of
price protection for the industry as was to be the case in
respect of jute in 1948. Up to 1958 cotton goods imports,
largely from developing Commonwealth countries, entered the
U.K. from these countries free of tariff or quota restrictions;
and only minor restrictions applied in respect of other
countries. A system of "voluntary limitation" operated from
early 1959, and was expanded in the early 1960's. Such arrangements were never, however, a major part of the U.K. government's policy in respect of the domestic cotton industry. The
Cotton Report of 1946 placed more emphasis upon (compulsory)
amalgamations and levy-financed machine redundancy and re-
equipment: schemes of which the industry had of course had
previous experience. It should be noted that the structure of
the cotton industry at this time was not unlike that of jute.
The market was dominated by a single large firm, J. & P.
Coats. There was a group of medium-sized firms, including
Fine Spinners & Doublers, and the Lancashire Cotton Corporation,
and a large "tail" of small firms. In contrast to the jute
industry, however, few of the large firms in cotton were
vertically integrated (Dennison, 1959).

The Working Party recommendations outlined above were in fact

the solution adopted by the government for the industry as,
after 1951, demand - particularly export demand - fell away.
Although legislation to implement the recommendations of the
Cotton Report was introduced in 1948, the most significant
scheme was that introduced by the 1959 Cotton Industry Act.
Under this the government bore two-thirds of the cost of
paying firms to scrap existing machinery, an industry levy
financing the remaining third. A similar compensation scheme
for redundant employees was entirely financed by a levy on
firms. The 1959 Act also made grants to firms for re-equipment. The impact of the Act upon the industry can be seen
from the following data.

TABLE 5.3   U.K. Cotton Industry

	1937	1959	1967
Employees ('000)	360	239	100
Spindles (m. ring equivalent)	26	15	4.5
Looms ('000)	520	220	92
Cloth output (m. yds.)	4,000	2,333	1,300

Source : Miles, C. (1968). Lancashire Textiles: A Case Study
         of Industrial Change. C.U.P., London. Ch.3.

The 1959 Cotton Industry Act was an important watershed for
the industry itself, and also a significant piece of government intervention in private industry. The scrapping compensation scheme was open for acceptance by the firms for only
two months - August and September 1959 - and was seen by the
government as a once-for-all piece of intervention in the
market. The government spent around £17m. in total for the
scrapping scheme; and around 50% of the firms in the industry
(accounting for some 75% of employment in 1959) took part in
it. The effect of the scrapping scheme was greatest in
respect of single process, small scale spinning firms, where
the number of such firms (having under 1,001 employees) fell
from 82 in 1959 to 40 in 1965; and although the scheme was
not as effective as might have been expected in eliminating
firms in the very smallest size category, the disappearance
of small, non-integrated firms did have the double effect of
increasing the proportion of output in the industry accounted
for by integrated firms (from 30% in 1959 to 41% in 1965),
and reducing the significance of smaller firms. As a proportion of total employment in the industry, firms employing
fewer than 1,001 employees fell from 55% in 1959 to 46% in
1964 (Miles, 1968, Appendix).   The net effect of the
scrapping scheme was that of the industry's April 1959
capacity, 48% of spinning spindles, 27% of doubling spindles,

and 38% of looms were scrapped. The re-equipment phase of the
1959 Act's provisions was expected to last until 1964. Here,
as might be expected from what was said before, the major up-
take of grants was by large, integrated firms. Single-process
firms accounted for only 31% of re-equipment expenditure, and
the average employment size of firms participating in the re-
equipment scheme was 594 compared with the industry average of
286.

As in the case of the jute industry, the cotton trade was subject to a number of outside influences over this period, which
make the impact of each separate change difficult to assess.
In 1959 alone the system of international trade protection was
changed, the 1959 Act began to have its effect, and the
industry's common minimum price agreement was terminated by
the Restrictive Practices Court. In addition, the years after
1959 witnessed continued secular decline of the industry,
further pressure from imports, and, as in the case of jute,
competition from synthetic fibres.

The 1959 Act and its implementation represented a major force
in the post-war history of the cotton industry. Its scrapping
provisions met with considerable response. As mentioned
above, almost half (48%) of the April 1959 installed spinning
plant was scrapped under the 1959 Act scheme; and the corresponding figures for doubling and for weaving were 27% and 38%.
The incidence of re-equipment, however, was low. Only around
half of the expenditure in this area expected by the Government and the industry was incurred (Miles, 1976 p.191); and
the reason most frequently given for this was the failure of
the Government at the same time to give the industry any
guarantee on import levels. This was a view concurred in by
a subsequent parliamentary inquiry into the impact of the
1959 Act (House of Commons, 1962). It was not until 1966
that a system of quantitative controls was applied to cotton
imports from countries other than Western Europe, North
America and Australia, and which therefore imposed the first
restrictions of any kind upon Hong Kong, India and Pakistan
which were responsible for the greatest proportion of U.K.
imports in this field. These quantitative controls operated
until they were entirely taken over by tariffs following
Britain's entry into the E.E.C.

In contrast to the jute industry, cotton textiles continued
to attract the attention of reports and enquiries until much
more recently. The most important of these was the 1969
Report by the Textile Council (1969). The 1969 Report
emphasised especially the need for restructuring and for a

more vigorous approach to marketing in the industry. In
particular it rejected any further scheme containing financial
incentives for scrapping plant. The Government followed this
analysis of the industry's problems by making funds available
to small and medium sized textile firms for re-equipment and
expansion through the Industrial Reorganisation Corporation.
At the other end of the size spectrum of firms the Government
in 1969 announced a general ban on mergers among the largest
firms in the industry; although it had to depart from this in
allowing the formation of Carrington Viyella in 1970 to
prevent the collapse of at least one of the firms.

The cotton industry, so far as changes in demand over the
last thirty years or so are concerned, has faced a situation
not dissimilar to that of jute. The two industries have,
however, responded and been treated by Governments in rather
different ways. In the case of cotton the response by the
Government in the post-war period, of which schemes it had
pre-war experience, was to encourage the industry to scrap old
plant and re-equip with new machinery, and in this respect the
1959 Act was partially successful. At the same time the
cotton industry was not until 1966 protected to any meaningful
extent from overseas competition by tariffs or other restrictions; and this absence of trade protection may have militated
against the complete effectiveness of the 1959 Act's inten-
tions. That is, although the 1959 Act provided some financial
incentive on the cost side for the industry to re-equip, it
may have been that this set of incentives was insufficient to
achieve its intended effect in a total environment of considerable uncertainty regarding the demand situation. It may thus
be that cost incentives without regard to demand conditions,
and tariff protection in particular, are not sufficient to
encourage re-equipment and the adoption of new technology.
The experience of the cotton industry indicates that tariff
protection and re-equipment subsidies are not necessarily
alternative means of promoting the survival of a particular
industry. Rather the experience suggests that cost
incentives must be accompanied by some assurances to the
industry regarding demand.

The jute industry's experience was the obverse of this. Jute
Control gave the industry trade protection; but there was no
provision for financial assistance for re-equipment.
Interestingly, nonetheless, the jute industry's record of
performance on re-equipment appears to have been good (see
Chapter 4 above) and part of the credit for this has been
accorded to the degree of certainty for producers in the
industry provided by Jute Control. It would seem, therefore,
that although there may have been some misallocation of

resources arising out of the system of Jute Control, so far
as offering a degree of trade protection to the industry and
encouraging it to re-equip and compete with imports is concerned Control was a more comprehensive system for achieving
such aims than the methods adopted in the case of cotton.
The 1959 Act offered the cotton industry only a financial incentive to scrap plant and re-equip. Jute Control, despite
not providing a monetary incentive to scrap old machinery and
instal new plant, in fact provided the reasonable certainty
of short-term future prospects which was evidently sufficient
to encourage a very creditable level of new investment in the
jute industry until the 1960's.

A further contrast between the two industries lies in the
fact that while the cotton industry has been in receipt of
continuing attention until comparatively recently, the trade
protection which jute enjoyed under Control was being phased
out by the mid 1960's, after which the industry received no
further special assistance from the Government. In some ways
this last contrast between the two industries - indicating
the greater and continuing degree of attention paid by
successive Governments to cotton in comparison with jute - is
itself not reflected in the apparent efficacy of the respective policies towards the two industries. Jute Control's
protection of the Dundee industry, without which there seems
to be no doubt the industry would not have survived in any
recognisable form in the 1950's, appears to have served its
purpose, and indeed was phased out as it became irrelevant
with the advent of polypropylene. In the case of cotton
there seems to be much less credit attributed to the various
scrapping and re-equipment schemes so far as their impact in
mitigating the effect of overseas trade on the industry is
concerned. Mrs. Miles, for example (1976, p.205), quotes
one senior civil servant as commenting, "My own personal
view is that developments in Lancashire have happened pretty
much as they would have anyway, even if there had not been
this government intervention"; and offers her own view that
"There is much truth in this verdict. ... The pace of decline
would probably have been much the same in the absence of any
adjustment assistance: there is no evidence to suggest that
the measures slowed it."

The comparative analysis of the recent experience of the jute
and cotton industries in the U.K. indicates that industries
in decline due to changes in technology and the impact of
import competition can be the subject of very different
Government policies. Equally the reaction of such industries
to factors affecting this decline and to Government policies
can differ significantly; and this fact again reinforces the

case made in the Introduction to this study for a case-by-case analysis of such situations.

DIVERSIFICATION

The term diversification has been used in this study to cover the broad corporate strategy on the part of individual businesses responding to rapid decline in their traditional market. Diversification thus covers the major part of market conduct or behaviour in this industry. It is an example, in this case, of resource reallocation in a market economy.

A number of points are worth making about the jute industry's response to the rapid decline in demand for its traditional product. In the first place the real pioneering work in the direction of developing textile applications was carried on outwith the Dundee industry. Plasticisers Ltd. (at the time a subsidiary of British Ropes (renamed Bridon), but now owned by Readicut International) is the firm normally credited with the initial development of polypropylene polymer extrusion and weaving. Such developments were, however, fairly rapidly adopted by two of the largest firms in the Dundee industry, Sidlaw and Low & Bonar, who, together with Plasticisers, were the initial shareholders in Polytape, and who were the equal co-owners of Synthetic Fabrics (Scotland). Plasticisers soon withdrew its very small shareholding from this consortium, and when Sidlaw withdrew in the mid 1970's this left Low & Bonar as the dominant integrated polypropylene textile manufacturer in Dundee. Low & Bonar was joined in this field fairly rapidly by other businesses large and small. Some of these operated on an integrated basis from an early stage, but a number of others were still at the end of our period of study (1977) simply weavers of tape. (A number of such businesses have since integrated backwards into extrusion either by acquiring an extruding subsidiary, or more commonly by purchasing extruding machinery.) Thus, as was suggested in Tables 3.1 and 3.2 in Chapter 3, the adoption of the "rival" product and technology was for most firms the natural response to the change in their market environment.

Although it would be difficult to estimate whether the Dundee jute industry firms responded as rapidly as possible to the opportunities of the new technology, it is worthwhile reiterating the point that the operation of Jute Control (albeit in diluted form throughout the 1960's) and the industry's own common pricing agreements probably distorted the introduction of polypropylene as a replacement yarn and fabric for jute. We have already commented on the fact that there appears to be evidence that the jute industry's raising of the price of its product above the level which would otherwise have existed not only denied customers (predominantly carpet manu-facturers) access to cheaper backing material, but also hastened the adoption by these same carpet manufacturers of polypropylene for both woven and tufted carpets compared with the situation in the United States of America.

The statistical analysis of diversification using company accounting data failed to reveal any significant differences in the performance of Diversified and Non-diversified firms over the period 1968-1977 in terms of profit performance (including maintenance of earlier average levels) or growth. There was, however, some evidence that diversification had reduced profit variability and that those firms which had diversified were initially larger in terms of sales (and also value added) than those which chose not to follow such a strategy. It has to be accepted, however, in the light of the circumstances of the case, that the lack of dramatically conclusive findings may be inevitable. Problems highlighted in this instance were the varied timing of the commencement of a diversification strategy on the part of the firms within our group of Diversified firms, the likely length of the time period over which the policy of diversification would yield returns in terms of increased profits etc., and the possible similarity of economic performance on the part of two groups of firms - one in the initial stages of diversification, the other continuing to operate in a declining market. Further-more, such findings as those in Chapter 3 are supported by those of a study of diversification across a larger number of companies (Grinyer, 1980). The finding of this wider study was that diversification as a corporate strategy did not con-tribute to enhanced profitability or growth or to reduced profit variability. Indeed, with particular relevance to our study, the authors of this analysis concluded on this point that "In general ... there is very little evidence that div-ersification is associated with, let alone causes, high performance in conditions of high technological change and market turbulence."

These results would seem to confirm our own findings that, regardless of the many possible reasons for adopting a strat-egy of diversification, it is a corporate policy which is unlikely to lead to significant gains in the short run for companies adopting it.

FINALE

The purpose of this last section is to offer some final comments on the study as a whole. These fall under the

headings of the usefulness of the structure-conduct-performance model, the issue of conclusions on resource allocation,
and the question of the balance between statistical analysis
and case-study material in this area of study.

Undoubtedly the structure-conduct-performance model has been
an extremely useful framework within which to examine this
industry over the past two decades. Without such a framework there is a real danger of accumulating a vast array of
quite disjointed material. Whether sufficient data has been
available for us to observe all of the interesting hypotheses
of the structure-conduct-performance model is more open to
doubt. Data on relative production costs, pricing and profit
margins broken down by product and by firms are simply not
available. Nonetheless it has been possible, for example, to
observe the behaviour of firms in terms of their trade
pricing and information agreements in the 1950's and 1960's.
It has also been interesting to identify those firms responsible for price leadership and technological change in the
industry, and to relate this to other dimensions of the firm's
conduct or position in the market. One particularly interesting feature within the structure-conduct-performance model
with reference to this study has been the role of barriers to
exit from the jute industry, and this too has been commented
upon.

Resource allocation is another topic on which one might have
been able to comment at greater length had more data been
available (eg. capital expenditure on various forms of plant
analysed by firm). Nonetheless our study has been quite a
vivid one of market forces at work forcing a reallocation of
resources across the industry in response to technological
change. We have been able to form an impression of the impact of Jute Control and the industry's trade pricing agreements at various stages of the market's development over the
last thirty years. The role of these seems to have changed
from one of ensuring the survival of the firms in the industry
in the 1950's in the face of Indian competition, to one in the
late 1960's of hastening the introduction of polypropylene in
the place of jute for tufted carpet primary backing through
overpricing jute relative to its cost in other similar
economies. One other area where we have been able to comment
on resource allocation relates to the adoption of new technology, where it was noted that the adoption of polypropylene
weaving and extruding was by no means the preserve of large
firms in the market.

Finally, we return to an issue raised in the Introduction to
this study: that of the balance to be struck in such an

analysis between case-study material and statistical
evidence. There is of course much to be said in favour of
presenting a statistical analysis of one's findings as we
have done in Chapter 4 of this work. Such analysis forces a
clarity of thought upon the researcher, and also leads to a
precise summary of results. It can even throw up results
which are not apparent at first sight from a glance at the
data. There are, however, two reservations regarding statistics which one must raise in respect of this study. In the
first place our population (and it is a population, not a
sample) of statistics is so modest in size that, even in
using nonparametric tests, one runs the risk of being accused
of using a statistical sledgehammer to crack a very small empirical nut. Second, case-study work is essential to analyse
aspects of an industry not susceptible to statistical
analysis, to clarify those cases where there is an absence of
expected statistically significant findings, and to explain
why statistically significant findings have arisen where they
have. Thus one would argue that Chapters 3 and 4 in this
study are complementary and not contradictory in their
approach to the study. Neither of them would be complete or
sufficient without the other. It is hoped that together they
have contributed to the economic analysis of the Dundee
industrial textiles industry which has been the purpose of
this study.

References

Caves, R.E. and M.E. Porter (1976). Barriers to exit. In
R.T. Masson and P.D. Qualls (Eds.), Essays on Industrial
Organization in Honor of Joe S. Bain. Ballinger, Cambridge,
Mass. pp. 39-69.

Corden, W.M. and G. Fels (Eds.) (1976). Public Assistance to
Industry: Protection and Subsidies in Britain and Germany.
Macmillan, London. pp.220-21.

Dennison, S.R. (1959). The cotton industry. In B. Tew and
R.F. Henderson (Eds.), Studies in Company Finance. C.U.P.,
Cambridge. pp.158-62.

Downie, J. (1958). The Competitive Process. Duckworth,
London. p.194.

Grinyer, P.H. and others (1980). Strategy, structure, the
environment and financial performance in 48 U.K. companies.
Acad. of Man. Jour., 23, 193-220.

House of Commons (1962). Fourth Report from the Estimates
Committee, Session 1961-62, Assistance to the Cotton Industry.
H.M.S.O., London. para. 26.

McDowall, S. and P. Draper (1978). Trade Adjustment and the British Jute Industry. Fraser of Allander Indtitute, Glasgow. p.3.

McDowall, S., P. Draper and T. McGuinness (1976). Protection, technological change and trade adjustment: the case of jute in Britain. O.D.I. Review, 1, 46-7.

Miles, C. (1968). Lancashire Textiles: A Case Study of Industrial Change. C.U.P., Cambridge.

Miles, C. (1976). Protection of the British textile industry. In W.M. Corden and G. Fels (Eds.) (1976).

Textile Council (1969). Cotton and Allied Textiles. Textile Council, Manchester. para. 96.

Tippett, L.H.C. (1969). A Portrait of the Lancashire Textile Industry. O.U.P., London. pp.1-4.

Author and Firm Index

Subject Index